MW01502601

WORLD PEACE

THROUGH THE TOWN HALL:

A STRATEGY FOR THE GLOBAL MOVEMENT

FOR A CULTURE OF PEACE

by David Adams

2009

To My Bahai brother Joe

Here is the best I can

do right now for a strategy!

Not easy but we've

got to try! David

© David Adams, 2009

Contact: david@cpnn-world.org

ISBN 1441480420
EAN-13: 9781441480422

Available for reading on-line or for mail-order at
http://culture-of-peace.info/books/worldpeace.html

Cover graphics come from the website
of the Culture of Peace News Network
http://cpnn-world.org

For the latest updates of information see
http://culture-of-peace.info/whatsnew

TABLE OF CONTENTS

INTRODUCTION

Soon the old system will collapse. The American Empire, the Great Powers, the globalized economy of capitalism, the very nation state itself, which have been developing over the course of history are not sustainable and all will fail. We are entering a period of dramatic historical change, and to keep us with events, his book will need to be updated on a regular basis (see http://culture-of-peace.info/whatsnew.html).

What will come next? Will there be only a temporary collapse followed by the reconstruction of an even more centralized power with states and empires based on the culture of war? This is what happened in the 1930's after the crash of 1929. Or will we seize the opportunity to create a new culture, a culture of peace? It is up to us.

The call for a Global Movement for a Culture of Peace has already been issued and taken up by 75 million people. In 1999, the UN General Assembly adopted a Declaration and Programme of Action on a Culture of Peace that called for the global movement. And in 2000, 75 million people signed the Manifesto 2000 (see page 29) committing themselves to promote a culture of peace in their daily lives, their families, their work and their communities.

However, as this is being written in 2009, the Global Movement for a Culture of Peace is still lacking a coherent strategy. During the decade since the call was first made by the UN, there has been some progress as reported by organizations of the civil society (see page 53), but great obstacles remain and the movement is still small and lacking direction.

The United Nations must play a key role in this strategy, but it must be transformed in order to do so.

As I write this introduction, sitting with my little computer on a bench across from Conference Room A at United Nations headquarters in New York, the corridor is jammed with people coming and going, a colorful parade of all races and nationalities, many of them wearing bright costumes, especially from Africa. It is the initial weeks of a new session and all the rooms along the corridor are busy with meetings.

Soon it will be twenty years since I left my university and went to work in the UN system to try to advance the cause of world peace.

Now, coming back to these halls, I still believe that it is through the United Nations that eventually we will be able to achieve world peace. However, I have been convinced by my experience with the UN and by my studies of history (Adams 2008) that this will not be possible so long as it is run by its Member States. Instead, we will have to take literally the words of the UN Charter written in 1945 which begins, "We the peoples", not "We the member states..."

"Think globally, act locally!" The old adage of the peace movement becomes more and more relevant. I have come to the conclusion, and hope to convince you, Dear Reader, of the same, that the United Nations will be able to help us achieve world peace, but this cannot happen until it is based on local governments instead of the Member States..

To make this case, your patience is requested to read through the following sections. They are written primarily for an audience of social movements, NGOs and local officials to explain how to create and operate a city culture of peace commission, but hopefully they will be of interest to all who hope for a better world.

In fact, work with social movements, NGOs and local officials is in dialogue with them, because they provide more than half of the input. Many of them have been working for a culture of peace and have accomplished much already, even if their achievements are known by another name. In this book, half of the dialogue is missing, since you the reader, with your own experiences and ideas, are not able to contribute. To do so, you are invited to take part in an interactive game on the Internet which covers some of the same ground (*www.culture-of-peace-game.org*).

Before going into the strategy, let me say what it is NOT. It is not the often-used strategy of having the town hall make pronouncements on international affairs, such as the legitimacy of particular wars, nuclear weapons or the national military budget. And it is not the simply the practice of "foreign aid" given directly from cities in the North to cities in the South. As the saying goes, "I've been there, done that." In fact, back in 1990 I published a small article in the short-lived US journal, the Bulletin of Municipal Foreign Policy, entitled "Planning for Peace in New Haven" which was concerned with the military budget. It was an interview with the chair of the newly-established New Haven Peace Commission about a local referendum, sponsored by the Commission, which called for cuts in the national military budget and the savings to be used for the needs of the cities. The referendum was approved by the voters by a 5-to-1 margin. Afterwards, as typical of these things, nothing further happened. The New Haven Peace Commission is now part of the global campaign of "Mayors for Peace" which concerns itself mostly with the question of nuclear weapons.   For most citizens in the cities concerned, the initiative does not seem relevant to their daily lives.

International solidarity of towns and cities is important and a chapter will be devoted to this topic. However, the time has come for a new basis of solidarity consisting of initiatives at the local level.

Therefore, a new strategy is proposed here. The old strategy was concerned with "peace" in the traditional sense of the term, being "the absence of war between nation-states." The old concept of peace was the period of time between wars when no particular war was being waged, although, of course, preparations were being made for the next war.   The new strategy proposed here is the development of a new culture and a new, alternative base of political power, a "culture of peace."

1) THE DIFFERENCE BETWEEN "PEACE" AND "CULTURE OF PEACE" AND A BRIEF HISTORY OF THE CULTURE OF WAR

At the present moment of history, war and peace (defined as the absence of war) are issues that cannot be decided by the town and city. Instead the power to make decisions about these issues is monopolized by the nation-state, with support from the various institutions allied with it, the arms industry, the mass media and even the educational systems, including universities. While towns and cities are powerless to make decisions on the culture of war, they suffer from it nonetheless.   The main task of the city is the well-being of its citizens, which requires a culture of peace. But what is this culture of peace?

It is not by accident that the term "culture of peace" originated at UNESCO, the United Nations Educational, Scientific and Cultural Organization, and that it originated in a meeting in Africa in 1989. UNESCO was established after World War II to ensure that there would never again be another world war.   It made a distinction between the old concept of peace between sovereign states and a new concept, as yet unnamed, of peace between peoples.   The preamble to the UNESCO constitution declared in 1946:

> "That a peace based exclusively upon the political and economic arrangements of governments would not be a peace which could secure the unanimous, lasting and sincere support of the peoples of the world, and that the peace must therefore be founded, if it is not to fail, upon the intellectual and moral solidarity of mankind."

It was not until 1989 that this concept was given the name of "culture of peace" in the final declaration of the International Congress on Peace in the Minds of Men, sponsored by UNESCO in Yamoussoukro, Cote d'Ivoire. The declaration called for the construction of "a new vision of peace culture based on the universal values of respect for life, liberty, justice, solidarity, tolerance, human rights and equality between women and men"

In 1992, UNESCO decided to undertake an "action programme for the culture of peace"   It was one of those crucial moments in world history when advances could be made because the old order was changing. UNESCO had been transformed by the success of national liberation movements into an organization with a new potential majority of votes from the countries of the South. The Cold War had ended with the collapse of the Soviet Union. The UN Security Council, freed from the Cold War vetoes of the

Soviet Union, had begun to undertake peacekeeping missions, with a new doctrine of intervention spelled out in the 1992 document "An Agenda for Peace." And perhaps, most important, Federico Mayor, a "dark-horse candidate", had been elected as Director-General of UNESCO. He was a man committed to the Constitutional mandate of the organization and to the newly-emerged nations of the south. Mr Mayor took up the culture of peace as his priority.

Details of this history are provided on my website at *Early History of the Culture of Peace: A Personal Memoire* (Adams 2003).

The UNESCO (1992) Action Programme for a Culture of Peace declared:

> "to construct peace in the minds of men - that is the mandate of UNESCO. Never before has our work been needed so much. The world has reached a turning-point in history. It is a moment of opportunity for global co-operation for peace. It is a moment that should not be lost. It has become clear that military force cannot solve the global problems of violence and injustice. Military force can only continue the vicious cycle... We need peace culture, not war culture..."

During the decade of the 1990's, with the support of Director-General Mayor, our culture of peace unit began to establish national programmes for a culture of peace in countries such as El Salvador, Mozambique, Philippines, and even Russia, but by the end of the decade these initiatives had failed due primarily to lack of support from the rich Member States. It became evident that they did not want to see a culture of peace developed in those countries. Then, in 1998 the UN General Assembly in New York, thanks to the initiative of countries from the South, declared the year 2000 as the International Year for the Culture of Peace and requested from UNESCO in Paris a draft Declaration and Programme of Action on a Culture of Peace.

The Declaration and Programme of Action on a Culture of Peace, adopted as Resolution A/53/243 by the United Nations General Assembly in 1999, includes the final definition of the culture of peace. It is in fact a "final definition" because once the United Nations adopts a declaration of this type, like the Universal Declaration of Human Rights, it becomes a permanent standard-setting document. New resolutions can be adopted later, but the initial declaration cannot be amended. The culture of peace is defined as "a set of values, attitudes, traditions and modes of behaviour and ways of life." Notice that "culture" is defined in the broad anthropological sense, not in the narrow popular sense restricted to music, dance, and the other arts.

Although the Declaration section was somewhat politicized by the diplomats (e.g. insisting that it would not apply to the internal policies of the Member States), the section on the Programme of Action retained intact the eight programme areas of a culture of peace. This was due to the consummate diplomacy of Ambassador Anwarul Chowdhury of Bangladesh who shepherded its passage through an unprecedented nine months of discussion and opposition.:

1) a culture of peace through education
2) sustainable economic and social development
3) respect for all human rights
4) equality between women and men
5) democratic participation
6) understanding, tolerance and solidarity
7) participatory communication and the free
   flow of information and knowledge

8) international peace and security [with a priority on disarmament]

It is important to recognize at this point that with the exception of the 8th programme area, all of the culture of peace areas apply as directly to the policies of the city as they do to the policies of the state. The 8th programme area can be interpreted as public safety and gun control at the local level, as well as networking with other cities for peace at an international level.

We had arrived at these eight programme areas as alternatives to the culture of war, in other words, replacing the culture of war in all its eight characteristics by a culture of peace. In an earlier resolution of 1998, the UN General Assembly had called for a transition from the culture of war and violence to a culture of peace and non-violence. However, in 1999, the European Union claimed "there is no culture of war" and forced the revision of the document, omitting any reference to it. In order to see the analysis based on the culture of war, one must go back to the original draft (United Nations, 1998) before it was "censored:"

1. "Education is the principle means of promoting a culture of peace ... The very concept of power needs to be transformed - from the logic of force and fear to the force of reason and love." [Although education for the culture of war and violence is not specifically mentioned here, it is inferred that it is based on force and fear, i.e. the basic qualities of terrorism.]

2. "sustainable human development for all ... This represents a major change in the concept of economic growth which, in the past, could be considered as benefiting from military

supremacy and structural violence and achieved at the expense of the vanquished and the weak."

3. "The elaboration and international acceptance of universal human rights, especially the Universal Declaration of Human Rights, has been one of the most important steps towards the transition from a culture of war and violence to a culture of peace and nonviolence. It calls for a transformation of values, attitudes and behaviours from whose which would benefit exclusively the clan, the tribe or the nation towards those which benefit the entire human family."

4. "equality between women and men ... can replace the historical inequality between men and women that has always characterized the culture of war and violence."

5. "democratic participation and governance ... the only way to replace the authoritarian structures of power which were created by and which have, in the past, sustained the culture of war and violence."

6. "There has never been a war without an 'enemy', and to abolish war, we must transcend and supersede enemy images with understanding, tolerance and solidarity among all peoples and cultures."

7. "participatory communication and the free flow and sharing of information and knowledge ... is needed to replace the secrecy and manipulation of information which characterize the culture of war."

8. "International peace and security, including disarmament". [It seemed so obvious that we did not bother to state that this is an alternative to the soldiers and weapons that are central to the culture of war.]

I have conducted an exercise dozens of times, deriving the culture of peace by defining first the characteristics of the culture of war and then specifying their alternatives. The exercise is a key part of the dialogue with local activists and elected officials in order to clarify the difference between peace and culture of peace, war and culture of war. And no matter where the exercise is done, whether in Japan or Korea, Malaysia or Egypt, Netherlands, France, Spain or England, Brazil or Mexico, Canada or the USA, the results come out the same. It turns out that the culture of war is universal and, by consequence, its opposite, the culture of peace, is also universal. The United Nations Declaration and Programme of Action on a Culture of Peace, like its predecessor, the Universal Declaration of Human Rights, is valid on all continents and in all societies. War, which is universal, is the tip of a universal iceberg, of which the submerged base is the culture of war.

A full understanding of the culture of war requires a detailed analysis of its evolution and history, beginning in human prehistory, examining the first recorded civilizations 5,000 years ago, and bringing up-to-date the continuing evolution of the nation-state. Although there are many histories of war, the account in Adams (2008) is the first account, as far as I know, of the history of the culture of war. As for a history of the culture of peace, that remains to be written in future years and by future generations, although I have imagined its beginnings in my utopian novella (Adams, 2009).

To understand the evolution and history of culture is a task that is not often undertaken. The laws of cultural evolution are similar although not identical to the laws of biological evolution. The best scientific formulation of this, in my opinion, is by the anthropologist Leslie A. White in his book *The Evolution of Culture* (1959).

"We may think of the culture of mankind as a whole, or of any distinguishable portion thereof, as a stream flowing down through time. Tools, implements, utensils, customs, codes, beliefs, rituals, art forms, etc., comprise this temporal flow, or process. It is an interactive process: each culture trait, or constellation of traits, acts and reacts upon others, forming from time to time new combinations and permutations. Novel syntheses of cultural elements we call inventions..."

"...The interrelationship of these elements and classes of elements and their integration into a single, coherent whole comprise the functions, or processes, of the cultural system..."

"For certain purposes and within certain limits, the culture of a particular tribe, or group of tribes, or the culture of a region may be considered as a system. Thus one might think of the culture of the Seneca tribe, or of the Iroquoian tribes, or of the Great Plains, or of western Europe as constituting a system. ... But the cultures of tribes or regions are not self-contained, closed systems in actuality, at all. They are constantly exposed to cultural influences, flowing in both directions with other cultures."

In the present book, the culture of war is considered in the framework of the preceding anthropological analysis: it is a cultural system that has evolved over the flow of time. Although at one time or another, some tribes or regions have been relatively independent from this culture, over the course of history most peoples have come under its influence. And, as we shall see, the system of nation-states has been, from the beginning, embedded within its context. Going back to seek its origins, we will consider it as a cultural invention with a certain usefulness at the time it was invented.

Also following White's analysis we see that the various components of the culture of war are all interrelated. As he says, "It is an interactive process: each culture trait, or constellation of traits, acts and reacts upon others." Hence, to give just one of many possible examples, the secrecy of the culture of war supports authoritarian control by allowing certain information to be held only by those in power, and both make possible the practice of warfare by concentrating the command structure in the hands of a few.

Cultural inventions are retained and diffused if they are useful, just as biological mutations are retained if they are useful. For example, pottery was a very successful invention in human history, as it enabled people to carry and store water and other liquids. The usefulness of pottery is immediately obvious on a day-to-day basis. But the usefulness of war and the culture of war has not always been evident.

Sometime the usefulness of a cultural invention, such as war, is difficult to determine because it occurs so rarely. Herein, lies a serious weakness in the scientific method which is designed to investigate frequent or easily-repeatable events. Science is based on repeatability; hence, a scientific article includes a methods section that allows other scientists to reproduce the observations or experiments, as well as a results section that submits the obtained data to statistical analysis. But events that occur very rarely and are not easily repeated, are not easy for science to deal with. In fact, during my 30 years of scientific work, I saw many unexplainable events in the laboratory that occurred only once. These could not be repeated; they could not be subjected to statistical analysis. Hence, it was not possible to study these events by the scientific method.

To illustrate this point, here is an example of a cultural trait for which the usefulness may be evident only once in many generations. The example is taken from animal behavior although it applies equally well to human behavior: the care of sick and elderly animals. As a college student, I heard from Professor John Buettner-Janusch, about his observations on a troop of baboons in Kenya at a time of extreme drought, the worst in 25 years. When the last water-hole dried up, the troop would have died except for an extremely old and infirm individual. He was the only one more than 25 years old. He set out across the parched land toward a distant location where he remembered the only water-hole that still contained water during the previous drought. The group survived thanks to the care they had given to this old individual enabling him to keep up with the troop's movements, sharing food with him, etc. Although such an even might not occur more often than once in 25 years, it was crucial for the survival of the entire group.

The culture of war in prehistory was such a cultural trait for which the usefulness was rarely evident. The evidence presented in Adams (2008) supports the theory that prehistoric warfare was useful when there was unpredicted drought or natural disaster so extreme that a tribe would perish if it did not succeed in raiding the food supplies of its neighbors. Since this might occur only once in many generations, its usefulness would not be immediately evident.   This is illustrated in Adams (2008) by taking as a model the description of the biological evolution of fire-resistant seeds.

Once the state was invented and began to dominate human history, warfare took on a new function, serving to protect and expand state power. This had three aspects, two external and one internal: externally to protect the state against invasion by another army or to conquer another people for plunder and/or slaves (later colonies); and internally as the last resort to suppress rebellion and revolution. The external functions may be frequent and evident, but the internal function may be less frequent and less evident, although no less important for the survival of the state.   The very threat of internal intervention may prevent rebellion, just as it is often argued that a strong military prevents more frequent invasions from external enemies.

War, both before and after the invention of the state, was the tip of a cultural "iceberg." The base of this "iceberg" was a culture that sustained and made possible the act of war when and if it became necessary.

The culture of war in prehistory, before the invention of the state, can only be reconstructed on the basis of fragmentary archaeological and indirect cross-cultural anthropological evidence.   The evidence suggests that it had at least six aspects:

1. warriors and weapons
2. identification of an "enemy"
3. authoritarian rule associated with military leadership
4. education of young men to be warriors
5. control of information through secrecy
6. male domination

The relation of warfare to the culture of war has been investigated through cross-cultural analysis of non-state societies. The relation of warriors and weapons and identification of an "enemy" to the practice of warfare are so evident that they do not require discussion. However, the other aspects of a culture of war, beginning with authoritarian governance and the socialization of young men to be aggressive, deserve careful consideration.

In non-state societies, the higher the frequency of warfare, the less democracy and the more authoritarian the governance, according to the studies of anthropologists Carol and Melvin Ember. Conversely, democratic participation is negatively correlated with warfare frequency. This is measured by the Embers in terms of checks on leaders' power, ease of removing leaders from power and extensiveness of participation, as described in their paper, *Making the World More Peaceful* (Ember and Ember 2001). See Adams (2008) for further details.

The education of young men to be aggressive also correlates with the frequency of warfare. This is true for both initiation rites of young warriors, according to Carol and Mel Ember (2007) and practice of violent team sports, according to Sipes (1973). The Embers provide a number of convincing arguments based on data from pacified societies that socialization for aggression is the consequence, not the cause of frequent warfare. Societies with frequent warfare undertake more training of their young men to be warriors, not vice versa. In their words, "male initiation ceremonies function as the equivalent of basic army training in non-state societies by taking boys or young men away from their families, isolating them from females, and subjecting them to traumatic and grueling conditions". There are many descriptions of warrior initiation rites. A lengthy description of one such rite as conducted by the Dugum Dani of New Guinea (Heider 1979) is provided in Adams (2008).

Although the question of secrecy has not been systematically investigated by cross-cultural anthropology, it is clear from all accounts of non-state warfare that secrecy is essential. It is essential because the deadly raids of the most serious warfare are carried out by surprise and face the great risk of ambush if the plans become known by the enemy.

It is the need for secrecy about war plans that can explain the male monopolization and exclusion of women from prehistoric warfare, and the consequent domination by men of all subsequent history. In fact, my own studies of brain research and animal behavior had convinced me that the male monopolization of warfare did not originate from men being more aggressive or from any particular difference in the brain of men and women, (Adams, 1992, *Biology does not make men more aggressive than women*).

It turns out on the basis of a scientific analysis that women were excluded early in prehistory from having any part in warfare because a woman's husband would be fighting on one side of a war and her father and brothers on the other side: hence, women could not be trusted. This was the result of the prevailing marriage systems that are called by anthropologists, "patrilocal exogamy". Exogamy is when one marries only outside the immediate village or tribe. Patrilocal is when the woman goes to live with the man. The evidence for this explanation of the monopolization of warfare by men was presented in my paper, *Why There Are So Few Women Warriors,* published in 1983 in the major journal of cross-cultural anthropology of that time, *Behavior Science Research.*

The culture of war was transformed by the invention of the state at the dawn of recorded history. In the empires that arose more or less independently in the different continents of the world (China, India, Mesopotamia, Egypt, Greece and Central America), we can already find a fully-developed culture of war described in their written records.

Details on the culture of war are available from the six major civilizations that first invented writing: Mesopotamia, Egypt, China, Greece and Rome, Hebrew civilization, and the ancient Central American civilization. They are remarkably similar in their culture of war. One ancient society, that of Crete, stands out as perhaps having been closer to a culture of peace. And the ancient civilizations of the Indus valley are more complex: the more ancient Harappan civilization may not have fully developed a culture of war, although later civilizations described in the epic Rigveda had arrived at it. There was a break in the Third Century BC when the emperor Ashoka of the Maurya Empire of the Indian subcontinent adopted the non-violence of the Buddhist religion for his kingdom.

The characteristics of the culture of war at the dawn of history, as described in the above societies, included the six characteristics inherited from earlier non-state societies (1-6 below) as well as 5 new characteristics (7-11) which made possible the expansion of empires and development of class-structured societies:

1. armies and armaments
2. identification of an "enemy"
3. authoritarian rule associated with military leadership
4. education of young men from the nobility to be warriors

     5. control of information through secrecy and
       propaganda
     6. male domination
     7. religious institutions that support the
       government and military
     8. artistic and literary glorification of military
       conquest
     9. wealth based on plunder and slavery
    10. economy based on exploitation (slaves, serfs,
       etc.)
    11. means to deter slave revolts and political
       dissidents including internal use of military
       power, prisons and executions.

Contemporary theories on the origin of the state, such as that of Carneiro (1970), often give a decisive role to warfare. Carneiro's analysis emphasizes the development of military leadership and a class-structured society based on slaves that were taken prisoner through warfare:

> "The expansion of successful states brought within their borders conquered peoples and territory which had to be administered. And it was the individuals who had distinguished themselves in war who were generally appointed to political office and assigned the task of carrying out this administration. Besides maintaining law and order and collecting taxes, the functions of this burgeoning class of administrators included mobilizing labor for building irrigation works, roads, fortresses, palaces, and temples. Thus, their functions helped to weld an assorted collection of petty states into a single integrated and centralized political unit.... These same individuals, who owed their improved social position to their exploits in war, became, along with the ruler and

his kinsmen, the nucleus of an upper class. A lower class in turn emerged from the prisoners taken in war and employed as servants and slaves by their captors. In this manner did war contribute to the rise of social classes."

The usefulness of war was greatly expanded and transformed by the state. Having made possible the accumulation of wealth in the form of land, riches and labor-power from slaves and other workers, war was used by the state for these purposes. As stated above in the culture of peace document that we sent from UNESCO to the UN General Assembly, "economic growth, in the past, could be considered as benefiting from military supremacy and structural violence and achieved at the expense of the vanquished and the weak."

From the beginning of the state, the usefulness of war was expanded into at least three new functions: 1) seizing land, wealth and slaves through the conquest of other peoples; 2) maintaining internal power against revolts of slaves and other oppressed peoples; and 3) defending the state against invasion by other military powers.

All of the various aspects of the culture of war at the dawn of history were inter-related, forming a single integrated system in which each aspect reinforced the others. The causal relationship is in both directions: warfare produces a culture of war and a culture of war produces war.

It is warfare that produces the culture of war. Warfare requires preparation in the form of armies and armaments. It is warfare, and nothing else (despite some claims of "human nature specialists") that leads to identification of an enemy. It is warfare, and nothing else, that makes possible plunder, slavery and colonialism; after all, no people ever volunteered to enter into slavery or colonialism if it was not backed by the force of arms. It is warfare, and nothing else, that requires the education of warriors. Further, the administration of the state is done by those who have distinguished themselves in war, hence the origin of authoritarian rule is associated with military leadership. To enforce internal order and prevent slave or other revolts in an economy based on exploitation, the state has sought a monopoly of force and potential violence, including associated institutions such as prisons, capital punishment, etc. The arts and religion have been employed by the state as an important arm of its culture of war, justifying the legitimacy of the state and its preparations for war. This serves the function of propaganda in its control of information. Central also to the conduct of warfare, the control of information also included secrecy about warfare planning as well as spying on the "enemy".

At the same time the culture of war is necessary for war. As we stated in the UNESCO document for the United Nations in 1998, without an enemy there can be no war. Without armaments and armies, no war. If no one obeys orders, there can be no war. And if war has not been profitable for slaves, colonies and neocolonialism, it probably would have disappeared long ago.

Perhaps the best illustration of the unity of the culture of war may be seen from the relative absence of all its attributes in the most exceptional case at the dawn of history, ancient Crete. According to the UNESCO history (1994), there were no fortifications and no glorification of war, although more recent archaeological excavations have turned up evidence of fortifications. Instead of gaining its wealth through conquest, Crete became wealthy through the maritime trade, using its great fleet of merchant ships throughout the Mediterranean, and these ships probably served as a defensive force to guard against any possible invasion.

The absence of warfare in ancient Crete allowed the development of a culture of peace in all its aspects. For example, women had more equality than in other ancient civilizations. According to the UNESCO history, "Cretan women took part in social and religious events and, furthermore, played an important part in society." Similarly, the state appears to have been less authoritarian than in other ancient civilizations. The role of the king was unlike that on the Greek mainland where "the Mycenean king, or annex, was required to be a great warrior ... In the Minoan states, the king is thought to have performed the functions of priest and judge but did not wield power of any note in other matters." The civilization of Ancient Crete did employ some slaves, although it appears that unlike in other empires, they were obtained through trade rather than military conquest.

The role of religion has been complex and often paradoxical throughout history,. Prior to the invention of the state, religious rituals might be used to invoke the help of the gods in warfare, but according to White in his *Evolution of Culture*, religion was not used to maintain internal power or to enforce the rules governing social relations. For example, according to White, "Virtually nowhere do we find that marriage or divorce is an affair of the gods in preliterate systems. Nor is the killing of a fellow tribesman, even a member of one's own family, an affair in which the gods have any concern..."

With the invention of the state, however, religion was appropriated by the state to provide it with legitimacy and to keep the citizenry in line through theology and rituals that installed obedience, docility and loyalty. White provides examples from the Incas, the ancient Egyptians, early Mesopotamia and ancient Sumer, Assyria and ancient India, as well as Greece and Rome (see Adams 2008).

At the same time, in reaction against the appropriation of religion by state power, there were movements throughout the world for new religions that were, at least in their origins, independent of the state and its culture of war. The period around 800-400 BC has been called the "Axial Age" (or "Pivotal Age") by the philosopher Karl Jaspers (1953). During this time, Confucius taught in China, the Siddhartha Gautama (Buddha) taught in India, Zoroastrianism arose in Persia and Jainism in India, the Upanishads were written in India, Elijah, Isaiah and Jeremiah prophesied in Israel, foreshadowing the life and teachings of Jesus and Mohammad at a later time.   In Greece, Socrates and Plato developed philosophy, which, although not a religion, has shared many of its values. These prophets were not affiliated with the emperors of the first empires. Instead, they preached individual morality and salvation, spirituality instead of wealth. Their ascetic lives, as well as the lives of their followers who were often wandering monks, provided an alternative culture to that of the warring empires that dominated the world at that time. Instead of war, the prophets sought to understand the meaning of life, to find truth through knowledge and spiritual discipline.

The culture of war has remained dominant throughout the 5,000 years of recorded history, through the rise and fall of empires, the period of history when Europe and Asia were over-run by warring herdsmen from Central Asia, the enslavement of Africans as the basis for a global economy, the period of colonialism and world wars, revolutionary wars and the Cold War, and the most recent neo-imperialism, so well described in the long description quoted from Kwame Nkrumah (1965) in Adams (2008).

Over the course of history, most aspects of the culture of war have remained as strong as ever. The description written above of the culture of war in the first empires of history applies to today's world with very little change, for example, substituting the word "workers" for "slaves."

The most important change in the culture of war in recent centuries has been the increased importance of the control of information through propaganda and secrecy, which serves to strengthen the culture of war in the face of the apparent decrease in authoritarian governance. This is best illustrated by consideration of the debate by many political scientists over the assertion that "democracies do not make war on other democracies."

Political scientists have made a case that democracy is increasing around the world, and that "democracies do not make war on other democracies." However, there is no evident decrease in the power of the culture of war throughout the world, or in the death and suffering that is caused by war and economic domination, or in the threat that new wars are on the horizon that could be even more terrible because of nuclear proliferation. How can this paradox be explained?

To some extent the paradox can be explained by the definitions used by political scientists. Hence, in their terms, if the US engages in war or the threat of war against Cuba, it doesn't count because Cuba is not considered democratic. And when the US engaged in the overthrow of the democratic government of Allende in Chile, it doesn't count because it was a secret war, not an overt public war. Perhaps their assertion should be rephrased as "democracies are not able to justify war against other democracies." After all, it is true that there is increasing democratic pressure against war. For example, when the US and its allies were mobilizing for the war in Iraq in 2003, there was an unprecedented outpouring of people onto the streets in anti-war demonstrations, over 10 million at least, and since then there are many cases where national elections see the defeat of candidates who have supported unpopular wars.

But the deep paradox is best understood in terms of the increasing role played by the combination of government secrecy and mass media propaganda that limit the effectiveness of democracy. Democracy cannot be effective if citizens do not have access to truthful information, and government secrecy in the name of "national security" is at an all-time high throughout the world. As we said in the draft culture of peace document sent by UNESCO to the General Assembly (United Nations, 1998):

> "It is vital to promote transparency in governance and economic decision-making and to look into the proliferation of secrecy justified in terms of 'national security', 'financial security', and 'economic competitiveness'. The question is to what extent this secrecy is compatible with the access to information necessary for democratic practice and social justice and whether, in some cases, instead of contributing to long-term security, it may conceal information about processes (ecological, financial, military, etc.) which are a potential threat to everyone and which need therefore to be addressed collectively."

Not surprisingly, the preceding paragraph was removed from the final adopted version at the demands of the European Union and their allies.

At the same time, the mass media is filled with propaganda that favors the culture of war and it fails to disseminate the voices of a culture of peace. Candidates that represent the powerful forces of societies are able to buy hundreds of millions of dollars of advertising and consequent free publicity on the "news programs" for their political campaigns, while those who do not represent these forces are excluded and are not heard by the voters. Decisions that support enemy images as well as actual decisions for war are often supported in the mass media by elaborate information and misinformation, while dissenting information is swamped or not presented at all.

I experienced firsthand the media bias for the culture of war in 1987 when we tried to get press coverage for the endorsement of the Seville Statement on Violence by the 65,000 member American Psychological Association (APA). As described in the next chapter, the Seville Statement was an important international statement by scientists that war is not part of human nature. Here is a description of the media blackout, as recounted in the Journal of Peace Research (Adams 1989):

"a press conference was organized at the APA convention in New York City where the endorsement was finalized, and over 400 press releases were sent out. Despite these releases, telephone calls, and personal contact with reporters in the press room, only four reporters showed up. They were out-numbered by APA presidents and past-presidents, not to mention representatives of other endorsing organizations. The four reporters were hardly a random sample: the APA Monitor (house organ of the Association), TASS from Moscow, ADN from East Germany, and the People's Daily World of the U.S. Communist Party. All four gave us well-written publicity, but they did not reach the audience we sought. One major news service told me on the telephone: 'Your Statement is not newsworthy, but call us back when you find the gene for war.'"

Although Science magazine represents all of the major scientific organizations of the United States they refused to publish information on the Seville Statement after it been endorsed by two of its constituent organizations, the American Psychological Association and American Anthropological Association. They even refused to publish a letter to the editor signed by the presidents of these very organizations!   As recounted in the Journal of Peace Research article (Adams 1989):

> "As it became obvious that most of the press was not going to attend the press conference, we drafted a 'letter to the editor' which was sent to the New York Times, Nature, and Science. The news editor of Science had been personally invited to cover the press conference but said that it was 'not newsworthy'. The letter called attention to the Seville Statement and its message and was signed by the presidents of the APA, the American Anthropological Association (which had also endorsed), and representatives of the International Council of Psychologists, Psychologists for Social Responsibility, International Society for Research on Aggression, and Society for Psychological Study of Social Issues. In response, we never received acknowledgements from the New York Times or Nature, and only a form letter of rejection from Science. Contacted by telephone, the letters' editor at Science said that the letter was 'too political'."

At the same time as Science magazine refused to cover the Seville Statement because it was "too political", they gave headline publicity to those who claim a genetic component of war, such as Napoleon Chagnon's claims about the Yanomamo Indians of the Amazon basin. Later it turns out that Chagnon's data may have been falsified (see the Seville Statement Newsletter, March 2003 at *www.culture-of-peace.info/SSOVnews303/page4.html*) although as far as I know this has never been acknowledged by Science magazine.

There are strong ties between the mass media, elected officials at the national level, and the arms industry. In the United States, one speaks not only of a "military-industrial complex," but also of a "military-industrial-congressional complex" and a "military-industrial-media complex." In addition to these overt relations, there are also covert relations between the arms trade and the lucrative trade in addictive drugs, relations which have often involved (secretly, of course) the highest levels of national governments. All of this is considered in detail in Adams (2008).

One also needs to ask even more profound questions about the nature of Western "democracy." This is being written during the euphoria following the election of Barack Obama as President of the United States. People are saying, "at last we have found a good leader". But this is troubling, because the American President is the commander-in-chief of the American empire. In fact, the "winner-take-all" structure of Western democracy plays into this concentration of power. Those who drafted the constitution after the American Revolution, realizing that "absolute power corrupts absolutely" and for this reason they wrote into the Constitution checks and balances between executive, legislative and judicial branches.

In sum, the culture of war is alive and well in today's world, even though the United Nations is forbidden to speak about it. But can we develop a culture of peace to replace it? This is the main question to be addressed in the succeeding chapters.

2) THE ROLE OF THE INDIVIDUAL IN THE CULTURE OF WAR AND CULTURE OF PEACE

I believe that history is in our hands, the hands of individuals like you and me. "Peace is in our hands" is the slogan that we adopted for the International Year for the Culture of Peace (the Year 2000). As said by the great anthropologist Margaret Mead, "Never doubt that a small group of thoughtful, committed citizens can change the world. Indeed, it's the only thing that ever has." Therefore, it is fitting that we begin our analysis with the role of the individual.

In fact, there really should be no border between psychology and anthropology or between the individual and culture as they are completely intertwined and inter-related. Culture is composed of individuals and it changes as individual consciousness changes. At the same time, the human being is the "cultural animal", and can only be understood in the context of his or her culture.

My study, *Psychology for Peace Activists* (Adams 1987), investigates the stages of consciousness development of peace activists, which usually passes through six stages, in more or less the same order. The data in the book show that these stages may occur at any point in life, from childhood to old age, which means that it is never too early or too late to develop consciousness, and that every person has the potential:

1) values
2) anger against injustice
3) action
4) affiliation
5) personal integration
6) and, in the case of the greatest peace activists, world-historic consciousness.

The initial stage, the stage of **values**, is the most basic, and hence, one can argue, the most important. It was this level that we put our greatest emphasis in the International Year for the Culture of Peace, circulating the Manifesto 2000 to be signed by individuals to work for a culture of peace in their everyday lives. The Manifesto was a translation of the eight programme areas of the culture of peace into six sets of values for everyday life.

<u>The Manifesto 2000</u>

Because the year 2000 must be a new beginning, an opportunity to transform - all together - the culture of war and violence into a culture of peace and non-violence.

Because this transformation demands the participation of each and every one of us, and must offer young people and future generations the values that can inspire them to shape a world based on justice, solidarity, liberty, dignity, harmony and prosperity for all.

Because the culture of peace can underpin sustainable development, environmental protection and the well-being of each person.

Because I am aware of my share of responsibility for the future of humanity, in particular to the children of today and tomorrow.

I pledge in my daily life, in my family, my work, my community, my country and my region, to:

Respect all life: Respect the life and dignity of each human being without discrimination or prejudice;

Reject violence: Practice active non-violence, rejecting violence in all its forms: physical, sexual, psychological, economical and social, in particular towards the most deprived and vulnerable such as children and adolescents;

Share with others: Share my time and material resources in a spirit of generosity to put an end to exclusion, injustice and political and economic oppression;

Listen to understand: Defend freedom of expression and cultural diversity, giving preference always to dialogue and listening without engaging in fanaticism, defamation and the rejection of others;

Preserve the planet: Promote consumer behaviour that is responsible and development practices that respect all forms of life and preserve the balance of nature on the planet;

Rediscover solidarity: Contribute to the development of my community, with the full participation of women and respect for

democratic principles, in order to create together
new forms of solidarity.

The Manifesto 2000 was signed by 75 million
people for the International Year for the Culture of Peace.
This was accomplished through the education and
mobilization of the vast network associated with UNESCO:
the National Commissions in every country; the UNESCO
field offices in many countries; the field offices of other
United Nations organizations and agencies; universities;
cities and towns, and the civil society organizations affiliated
with UNESCO and the UN. They, in turn, educated and
mobilized their constituencies.

If we could have continued the campaign beyond the
Year 2000, we could have achieved a great step forward
towards a culture of peace. But it wasn't to be. Under
pressure from Europe and the US and their allies, the
campaign was ended and the culture of peace initiatives were
deprived of funding and staff.

The second stage of consciousness development, as
seen in the lives of great peace activists, is **anger**. This was
a great surprise to me, as it has been to many of my readers.
Reading one autobiography after another, one finds
quotations like the following from the autobiography of
Nelson Mandela (1994):

> "I had no epiphany, no singular revelation, no
> moment of truth, but a steady accumulation of a
> thousand slights, a thousand indignities and a
> thousand unremembered moments produced in
> me an anger, a rebelliousness, a desire to fight
> the system that imprisoned my people. There
> was no particular day on which I said,
> Henceforth I will devote myself to the liberation

> of my people; instead, I simply found myself doing so, and could not do otherwise."

According to Martin Luther King, Jr (1968), the harnessing of anger is the greatest of tasks:

> "The supreme task is to organize and unite people so that their anger becomes a transforming force."

Gandhi (1929) also talks about the harnessing of anger as a powerful force for justice:

> "I have learned through bitter experience the one supreme lesson to conserve my anger, and as heat conserved is transmuted into energy, even so, our anger controlled can be transmuted into a power which can move the world."

Anger, as it turns out from my studies of aggressive behavior, is the natural human response to perceived injustice. This is discussed in detail from a scientific perspective in my book *The Aggression Systems* (Adams 2003), that is available on the Internet.

On the other hand in my studies, I have found, again to my initial surprise, that anger is not an important motivation for warriors. Instead, it turns out that the training of warriors is designed to enable them to ignore their emotions, especially fear, and to act rationally. This is described for the present day in the book *On Killing: The Psychological Cost of Learning to Kill in War and Society* by Lieutenant Colonel Dave Grossman of the U.S. Army (1995). And apparently it has always been the case, as shown in my analysis of the warfare by non-state societies in New Guinea (Adams, 1984, *There is no instinct for war*). A good warrior follows orders and does not get angry at his superior officer, or, in the case of the superior officer, he should not get angry at the men under his charge. For example, at one point during the first Iraq war, it was said that the supreme commander General Schwarzkopf was losing his temper against his officers so often that morale was being undermined and the Secretary of Defense, Dick Cheney, had to make a special trip to Saudi Arabia to tell him the equivalent of "One more temper tantrum and you're fired."

Of course, we must not forget that anger can be a destructive as well as a constructive motivation in the lives of individuals. Learning when and how to express anger needs to be an important part of the education of every person, in order to be able to harness the emotions for a productive life. This is especially a challenge for social justice movements. These movements attract new members who are full of righteous indignation against injustice. Thus, they have a higher, not a lower, proportion of "angry people" than in the general population. Unless these movements teach their members how to manage their anger and harness it to constructive action, they face a serious risk of being torn apart by disputes.

There is another related risk, more subtle, that is borne by social justice movements. Many who come to these movements, realizing that they have a high level of anger are so afraid of their own anger that they are greatly inhibited in their actions, fearing that they may offend others. These activists often turn to meditation and other forms of self-discipline, sometimes to the point that they are unable to act freely or to work well with others,

Ironically, the harnessing of "righteous indignation" was a key part of educational systems in the early years of America when education was run by the church. It was only after education came under control of the state after the

American Civil War that anger was said to be "bad" and all anger was to be suppressed. This is described in detail in the book, *Anger: The Struggle for Emotional Control in America's History* (Stearns and Stearns, 1989). It is probably not by accident that this period, around the 1870s corresponded to what was called the "industrial wars" when thousands of federal troops and National Guard were called out to suppress the strikes by industrial workers. It was at this time that the National Guard was founded and headed by the industrialists as described in *Internal Military Interventions in the United States* (Adams 1995) which is available on my Internet website.

For many years I was greatly influenced by the fallacy that war is based on anger, and therefore part of human nature. My work in brain research, investigating the mechanisms of aggressive behavior, was originally motivated by the mistaken belief that this would contribute to world peace by discovering an instinctive source of war. By the time I wrote a definitive scientific review of the subject after more than a decade of work (Brain Mechanisms for Offense, Defense and Submission, Behavioral and Brain Sciences, 1979), I had come to realize that my basic premise was wrong. The final words of that scientific paper say that:

> "Human aggression has been transformed by many cultural factors such as the development of institutions and economic systems and the elaboration of motor patterns with tools and language. Knowing this, we have a moral obligation to avoid oversimplified phylogenetic extrapolations (which may be 'particularly provocative' as noted by Paul Brain), and we should make I clear that such human phenomena as crime, revolution, and war are not the inevitable results of neural circuitry."

Over the course of my studies it became clear that anger is not the basis for warfare. Warfare, and even more so, the culture of war that underlies it, is a cultural, not a biological phenomenon. The "evolution of war and the culture of war" (Adams, 2008), refers to cultural evolution and not biological evolution.

In a scientific study conducted with the help of one of my students at the university (Adams and Bosch, 1987), we showed how the belief that war is part of human nature makes people less likely to take action for peace because they believe that the cause is hopeless. In their thinking, since war is part of human nature, it is therefore inevitable and cannot be changed. On the other hand, those who understand that war is not part of human nature are more likely to take action because they believe that their actions can have an effect and help to prevent war.

Recognizing this as an important issue, I worked with the International Society for Research on Aggression to organize a high-level conference of scientists from around the world in 1986 in Seville, Spain, to answer the question, "Is war part of human nature?" The scientists came from all the relevant biological and social sciences: genetics, brain research, animal behavior, sociology, psychology and anthropology. We issued the Seville Statement on Violence (Adams 1989, 1991), which considers and rejects the following five arguments:

> * that we have inherited a tendency to make war from our animal ancestors.

> * that war or any other violent behavior is genetically programmed into our human nature.

* that in the course of human evolution there has been a selection for aggressive behavior more than for other kinds of behavior.

* that humans have a 'violent brain'.

* that war is caused by 'instinct' or any single motivation.

The scientists concluded at Seville that "the same species that invented war is capable of inventing peace" paraphrasing a statement published a generation earlier by the great anthropologist Margaret Mead.

The Seville Statement on Violence was subsequently endorsed by the United Nations Educational, Scientific and Cultural Organization, as well as many scientific organizations including the American Anthropological, Psychological and Sociological Associations, and it was widely diffused and discussed. In the years since the Seville Statement was published, there has been little change in the scientific evidence, as documented in the newsletter of the Seville Statement on the Internet at *www.culture-of-peace.info/SSOVnews303/page2.html* .

Action is obviously a key stage of the consciousness development of activists. The details of this are made clear from my studies of consciousness development. However, one seeks in vain in most psychology textbooks and university courses for the psychology of action! Instead, consciousness is usually treated by academic psychology in terms of passivity: studies of sleep and dreaming, drugs and yoga meditation, and attitude change that is described in terms of an "outside" force changing the attitudes of an otherwise passive subject.

An appropriate view of action is taken by the Brazilian educator, Paulo Freire (1968) in his important book, *Pedagogy of the Oppressed.* Freire considers that action is essential to effective education, which he calls "problem-posing education" as opposed to the "banking concept of education" that is used by entrenched powers and bureaucracies to keep people passive:

> "Problem-posing education bases itself on creativity and stimulates true reflection and action upon reality, thereby responding to the vocation of men as beings who are authentic only when engaged in inquiry and creative transformation. In sum: banking theory and practice, as immobilizing and fixating forces, fail to acknowledge men as historical beings; problem-posing theory and practice take man's historicity as their starting point."

Affiliation is the next stage after action. Quite simply, activists find that they are more effective when they work in a group rather than alone. As the great peace activist Eugene Victor Debs concluded at the end of his life, "Unorganized you are helpless, you are held in contempt. Power comes through unity." (See Adams 1987).

Affiliation, more than any other step, requires the learning of psychological skills. From the study of autobiographies, it may be seen that these skills include the willingness to compromise and accept group discipline, the courage to give of oneself and to accept criticism, while curbing the excessive criticism of others, and the patience to help others develop their own unique powers of thought, feelings and actions. The principle of "listen to understand" is essential (See the Manifesto 2000 above). Given the emphasis on individualism in the United States and other

Northern countries, it is not surprising that introductory psychology books give almost no space to these skills.

It is clear that world peace cannot be attained quickly, and that the task is long-term. A peace activist must be ready to work throughout an entire lifetime in order to achieve some progress. It follows that effective peace activists are those who manage to integrate their activism with the other aspects of their life, their family life and earning a living. This is difficult because there is very little money available to pay people to work for peace, and for most activists, their work for peace must be in addition to an income-generating job.

As far as consciousness development is concerned, it makes little difference what organization a person joins, as the same psychological skills are needed and can be developed. However, the long-term effectiveness of the individual's efforts depends on the relation of his/her affiliations to historical forces on a global scale. This is what I have called "**world-historic consciousness**" in *Psychology for Peace Activists* (Adams 1987). The present book attempts to discover some of the important forces at this moment of history that can help people develop world-historic consciousness and guide their decisions and affiliations to be most effective.

It appears that we are entering into a period of history when the principles and possibilities of world-historic consciousness become evident to millions of people and social progress can become radical and revolutionary. In such a time, there can be an additional step in consciousness development which I have called "**vision**", the wide-spread sharing of the world-historic consciousness of the leaders of the movement. However, if the ground has not been prepared in advance, and if the "vision" is not widely available, it may be too late to mobilize the masses of people for progressive social change. I hope that this book will contribute to the development of the vision that is needed.

3) WHY THE NATION-STATE CANNOT CREATE A CULTURE OF PEACE

Traditionally, it has been thought that world peace could be achieved through the nation-states and their organization on a global basis through the United Nations, or, earlier, the League of Nations. And in fact, that was my assumption in 1992 when going to work at the Paris headquarters of UNESCO, the United Nations Educational, Scientific and Cultural Organization.

However, as mentioned in the beginning of this book, I have come to a different conclusion on the basis of my experience in the United Nations system, as well as my studies of the history of the culture of war as detailed in Adams (2008).

The problem of the state is of central importance for all who are working for world peace. Most peace initiatives are directed at changing the policies of the nation-states and the United Nations in the belief that this is the "fulcrum" or "lever" where it will be possible to make the historical transition from the culture of war to a culture of peace. However, if the nation-state, by its very nature, cannot make peace, then there needs to be a radical change in the strategy and tactics of all who are working for peace. Because the question is so important, we need to take the time here to explore it in some detail.

The entire cultural evolution and history of the culture of war since the invention of the state, as described in Adams (2008), can be summarized as the state's progressive monopolization and refinement of the culture of war. The popular film genre, the American Western movie, can be seen as an allegory of the state's monopolization of killing. In a typical movie, there is killing or threats of killing in the beginning of the film by outlaws, American Indians, or so-called citizen posses that take the law into their own hands. Then the sheriff arrives from the East, representing the state, and he takes command of the situation by imposing "the law," which means that he, and only he, in the name of the state, can decide who can administer "justice," i.e. who has the right to kill or threaten to kill.

In recent history, the state has succeeded to such an extent in its monopolization of killing and violence that we take it for granted. The very definition of the state for sociologists like Max Weber is based on warfare and the monopoly of force. His definition of the state is the organization that has a "monopoly on the legitimate use of physical force within a given territory" (Weber 1921). The definition of the "failed state" similarly depends on the monopoly of force, in this case, a failed state is one that has lost the monopoly of force.

At the United Nations in 1999, there was a remarkable moment when the draft culture of peace resolution that we had prepared at UNESCO was considered during informal sessions. The original draft had mentioned a "human right to peace" (Roche 2003). According to the notes taken by the UNESCO observer (See Adams 2003), "the U.S. delegate said that peace should not be elevated to the category of human right, otherwise it will be very difficult to start a war." The observer was so astonished that she asked the U.S. delegate to repeat his remark. "Yes," he said, "peace should not be elevated to the category of human right, otherwise it will be very difficult to start a war."

The countries of the European Union were similarly opposed to the human right to peace, although not as bluntly clearly stated as by the Americans, in the debate on this matter in the Fifth Commission of the UNESCO General Conference.. No official notes were taken at that Commission, but I took notes personally for the Director-General which may be found on my Internet website (see UNESCO 1999).

The human right to peace would deny the fundamental right of the state which has always been and continues to be the right to make war. This includes the right of the state to make war internally as well as externally. The message of the Europeans and Americans at the UN in 1999 was that the state is not going to give up this "right".

In fact, there has been no decrease in the state's preparations for war, both external war and internal war, in recent history. Most states, and their citizenry, speak constantly of their "enemies". The remarks by the recent U.S. President George W. Bush about its enemies constituting an "axis of evil" are no exception. The buildup of armaments and armies, which many thought would decrease after the end of the Cold War, have returned to the highest levels in history. Nuclear arms and their continued proliferation have added an especially dangerous dimension with the potential to destroy all life on the planet.

The priority devoted by the state to the military can be measured to some extent by its military spending. Here is a summary of national military expenditures in 1999 as published by the U.S. Department of State (2001). This is the most recent data I can find that shows military spending as a percentage of central government expenditures. These figures range from 4.2 to 22.4 percent, and they are probably underestimates. For example, according to the Friends Committee on National Legislation, in 2007 the U.S. government devoted 29% of its budget to current military spending and another 14% to debt payment for past military spending, a total of 43%, much greater than the 15.7% admitted in the official government figures. Much of the difference comes from U.S. government insistence on including social security entitlements as part of central government expenditures, even though it is simply reimbursing the investments that have been made by the citizen payments.

All states: 10.1%
Selected states
Russia 22.4%
China 22.2%
United States: 15.7%
United Kingdom 6.9%
France 5.9% (estimated)

Regions:
Middle East 21.4%
South Asia 16.1%
North America 14.6%
Africa 14.0%
East Asia 12.7%
Central Asia and Caucasus 9.2%
South America 7.6%
Oceania 7.0%
Europe 6.3%
Central America 4.2%

It is not just war, but more generally the culture of war that has become the monopoly of the state. Going down the eight characteristics one by one, we see that each has become more and more under the control of the state.

Perhaps the most remarkable is the control of information. As discussed in Adams (2008), the state has increased its domain of secrecy and its manipulation of the media. Also, as discussed earlier, the gains in democratic participation have been to a great extent offset by this increase in secrecy and propaganda.

The key to the culture of war is the labeling of an enemy. It was a remarkable moment when Mikhail Gorbachev, Premier of the Soviet Union, told President Ronald Reagan of the United States, "I am going to deprive you of your enemy." And indeed, the CIA had to get busy quickly to identify a new enemy for the American state. This was effectively accomplished by Professor Samuel Huntington and his thinktank at Harvard, who identified the new enemy as Islam in the celebrated essay on "Clash of Civilizations." Later, in 2001, the attack on the World Trade Center played into the hands of this new enemy image.

One might hope that adherence to the Universal Declaration of Human Rights would reduce war and the culture of war, but unfortunately, we see that countries of the North increasingly claim that their military interventions in the South are carried out in order to "defend human rights" in those countries.

There does seem to be a certain reduction in the male supremacy at the level of some states, but the reduction remains small in comparison to the continuing male dominance in the culture of war.

As for the nature of economic development, it remains firmly in control of the culture of war. One figure is clear from the annual United Nations Human Development Reports, the rich and powerful are getting richer and the poor and powerless are getting poorer, both within and between countries. There is increasing attention, now reaching to the level of the state, to the need for sustainable development, expressed in terms of concern about global warming, but the problem of increasing inequality of wealth and power, which is no less dangerous for the future of humanity, gets no effective attention from the state.   A few states devote a substantial sum to development aid projects, but the effectiveness of this aid is swamped by the profit-oriented practices of global business as well as corruption in donors and in the countries where the aid is received.

As for armaments, it is a case of the foxes guarding the chickens.   The five permanent members of the Security Council, responsible for disarmament at the United Nations, are the five great nuclear powers, and they show no signs of giving this up.   If anything, they are tending to promote nuclear arms among their allies, for example, the United States in the case of India.

Educational systems are increasingly controlled by the state, which gives the state more power to ensure that the curricula continue to teach that history is essentially the history of military victories and that power comes ultimately from force.   On the brighter side, Spain has recently adopted a national law to promote the teaching of the culture of peace in schools and hopefully this will provide a precedent to other states.

The more I investigate these matters, the more I am convinced that **internal war** rather than external war is the aspect that is most critical for the state.   Protection from external war could, in theory, be provided by the United Nations.   The United Nations condemns the conquest of one state by another, and the UN could be strengthened to provide the defense for states against being invaded by others.   What is at stake, instead, is the internal function of war, and in this case the United Nations has no jurisdiction. The United Nations Charter was written so as to forbid interference in the "internal affairs" of its Member States.

Internal war remains a taboo topic, even though it is crucial for understanding the relation of the state to the culture of war since internal war is required by the state, as a last resort, to maintain power and wealth. Over the course of history the systems of power and wealth have gone through a number of important transformations; from the slavery of the Greek and Roman and Islamic empires to the feudalism of medieval Europe to the enslavement of Africans in the New World colonies to the classic colonialism of the European powers and more recently to the exploitation on a global scale ("globalization") of industrial and agricultural wage workers under neo-colonialism.

Looking historically at the case of the United States, we see that, in the early days of the republic, internal intervention was used most often to seize land from the indigenous peoples in the West and to prevent slaves from rebelling in the South. The latter is described in my article, *Internal Military Interventions in the United States*: (Adams 1995).

> "The South was an armed camp for the purpose of enforcing slavery prior to the Civil War. In his survey of American Negro slave revolts, Aptheker (1943) found records of about 250 revolts and conspiracies, but said that this was no doubt an underestimate. Most of the revolts were suppressed by state militia, for which records are not readily available. In addition to suppressing revolts, the military enforced a state of martial law. According to Mahon (1983) in his History of the Militia and the National Guard, before the U.S. Revolution, 'the primary mission of the slave states' militia increasingly became the slave patrol' (p. 22) and after the revolution, 'the slave states continued to require

militiamen to do patrol duty to discourage slave insurrections' (p. 54).

The militarization of Southern cities was described by F. L. Olmstead in the late 1850s, as quoted by Aptheker (1943, p. 69):"

"'...police machinery such as you never find in towns under free government: citadels, sentries, passports, grapeshotted cannon, and daily public whippings. ..more than half of the inhabitants of this town were subject to arrest, imprisonment and barbarous punishment if found in the streets without a passport after the evening 'gunfire'. Similar precautions and similar customs may be discovered in every large town in the South. ..a military - organization which is invested with more arbitrary and cruel power than any police in Europe.'"

Although slavery was abolished in most countries by the end of the 19th Century, its place was taken by the exploitation of industrial and agricultural wage workers. At that point the internal culture of war was transformed in order to prevent and suppress workers' strikes, revolts and revolutions, as described for the United States in my article on internal military interventions:

"The strike wave of 1877 transformed internal military intervention in the USA into industrial warfare. It began with a railroad strike in West Virginia, which spread throughout the industrial states. Before it was over, 45,000 militia had been called into action, along with 2,000 federal troops on active duty and practically the entire U.S. Army on alert (Riker, 1957, pp. 47-48). To realize the scope of this mobilization, one needs to know that according to Riker there were only 47,000 militia used during the entire Civil War, and the size of the entire U.S. Army around 1877 was 25,000 (p. 41). From 1877 to 1900, the U.S. Army was used extensively in labor disputes and a shared interest developed between the officer corps and U.S. industrialists (Cooper, 1980).

The 1877 intervention gave birth to the modern National Guard. This point is agreed upon by the principal histories of the Guard (Derthick, 1965; Mahon, 1983; and Riker, 1957). As Riker documents in detail, not only did all of the states establish their National Guard at that time, but also the appropriations of the new Guard were almost perfectly correlated with the number of strikers in that state. He concludes that 'in short it is reasonable to infer that the primary motive for the revival of the militia was a felt need for an industrial police' (p. 55)."

In recent years there has been a convergence of neo-colonialism and the capitalist exploitation of industrial and agricultural wage workers. Industrial enterprises in the North have largely re-located into countries of the South, decreasing the industrial class struggle within the North and re-locating it to the South.

The use of the military for internal control has changed but not diminished in recent centuries. As mentioned above it has been used especially in the United States (and presumably other capitalist countries although data are not available) for the control of industrial workers. It has also been used for the prevention and suppression of revolutionary movements; for example, the development and frequent deployment of the CRS in France, an internal military force developed after the student rebellion of 1968 which threatened at the time to be joined by a workers' revolution as well. On the other side, newly established revolutionary governments also used the military to prevent counter-revolution, and to establish a chain of command throughout the country to replace previous mechanism of capitalism or feudalism. In the newly revolutionary China, the power base of the Communist Party and the government has been the Red Army. In the early days of the Soviet Union, Trotsky proposed that industrial production be organized primarily on the basis of military forced labor camps, and later Stalin began to carry this out. Paradoxically, when the Soviet Empire finally crashed in 1989 the military stayed in its barracks and did not intervene.

In the United States during the period 1886-1990 there have been 18 interventions and 12,000 troops per year, on average, against striking workers, urban riots, etc. This is detailed in my 1995 article mentioned above on *Internal Military Interventions in the United States*. I am not aware of systematic data for other countries or for the U.S. in the years since 1990.

Discussion of the internal culture of war remains a taboo topic even now as we enter the 21st Century. At the level of contemporary diplomatic discourse the taboo is total. Nation states consider that internal military intervention is a matter that is not appropriate for inter-governmental forums such as the United Nations. In fact, a special article was included in the UN Charter that forbids the UN from discussing the internal affairs of Member States:

> "Article 2.7: Nothing contained in the present Charter shall authorize the United Nations to

intervene in matters which are essentially within the domestic jurisdiction of any state...."

One is reminded of this taboo in considering, as described earlier, how the European Union demanded that all reference to the culture of war must be removed from culture of peace resolution adopted by the UN General Assembly in 1999.

Extreme examples of the taboo during the 20th Century are provided by Nazi Germany and Soviet Russia during the 1930's. Each had extensive systems of internal prison camps that could not be discussed publicly in those countries. Instead, all attention was focused on military confrontation with external enemies.

A less extreme example, but no less instructive, is the McCarthy period of U.S. history as described in my history of internal U.S. military interventions mentioned above. The emphasis on the military buildup during the Cold War, the labeling of an external enemy and the claims of extensive spying for this enemy functioned as the cover for internal repression of a militant trade union movement influenced by communist ideology, a repression that was difficult to discuss in public. Notice that here we are not talking about *internal war* as such, but rather the *internal culture of war*.

We have concentrated here on internal culture of war in the United States, but readers from other regions such as Latin America and Eastern Europe will have no difficulty in recognizing this dynamic in their recent history.

Discussion of internal culture of war is not only taboo at the diplomatic and political levels, but also in the mass media and academic institutions. For example, the analysis of U.S. internal military interventions in my 1995 article in the Journal of Peace Research points out the lack of attention to this topic:

> "The unchanging rate of internal military intervention in the USA and the lack of attention to such intervention in the literature on war and peace are in striking contrast to the rapid changes in other aspects of war and peace. It is argued here that this reflects an oversight which peace researchers and activists should address in the coming years."

Since the paper was published in 1995, the topic remains taboo. During the intervening twelve years, there have been only four academic references to the paper according to the Social Science Citation Index, even though it was published in a prestigious journal that one would expect relevant researchers to read. Nor have other academicians taken up the challenge independently.

It can be concluded from all of the preceding that the state cannot promote a culture of peace as long as it maintains a military force to protect and preserve in the last resort the inequities of wealth and power that it represents. At the present time, this question, the issue of internal military intervention, is rarely discussed, let alone addressed in an effective way.

Other great peace leaders have come to similar conclusions about the impossibility of arriving at peace through the state. Gandhi said the following in an interview with Nirmal Kumar Bose published in Modern Review, October 1935 and reprinted in UNESCO (1960):

> "The State represents violence in a concentrated and organized form. The individual has a soul, but as the State is a soulless machine, it can

> never be weaned from violence to which it owes its very existence. ... It is my firm conviction that if the State suppressed capitalism by violence, it will be caught in the coil of violence itself and fail to develop non-violence at any time."

And Johan Galtung (1996) has come to a similar conclusion in recent years, calling the state "basically incompatible with peace":

> "One reason why the state system today is basically incompatible with peace lies in the state patriarchy, in the arrogance and secrecy, in the *causa sua* mentality of being their own cause not moved by anybody else (and certainly not by democracy), in having a monopoly on the ultimate means of violence and being prone to use them ('to the man with a hammer the world looks like a nail'). All this is bad enough, even if generally less pronounced in smaller states, more in the larger ones, and even more so in super-states.
>
> "But in addition states are also sustaining themselves by a specific belief system that runs roughly as follows:
>
> *   the world system is basically a system of states ..."
>
> "* the sum of mutually adjusted state interests is the world and human interests (like male interests = human interests)."
>
> "...Both are blatantly wrong..."

4) THE IMPORTANT ROLE OF CIVIL SOCIETY IN CREATING A CULTURE OF PEACE

In 1998, realizing that the powerful states would oppose the culture of peace, we proposed in the draft Programme of Action on a Culture of Peace, that it should be promoted by a Global Movement for a Culture of Peace including not only the United Nations and its Member States, but also the civil society. This provision remained intact in the resolution that was finally adopted (United Nations 1999), and it is apparently the only time that the UN General Assembly ever called for a "*global movement*" (bold italics added):

> 2. Member States are encouraged to take actions for promoting a culture of peace at the national level as well as at the regional and international levels.
> 3. Civil society should be involved at the local, regional and national levels to widen the scope of activities on a culture of peace.
> 4. The United Nations system should strengthen its ongoing efforts to promote a culture of peace.
> 5. The United Nations Educational, Scientific and Cultural Organization should continue to play its important role in and make major contributions to the promotion of a culture of peace.
> 6. Partnerships between and among the various actors as set out in the Declaration should be encouraged and strengthened for a *global movement* for a culture of peace.
> 7. A culture of peace could be promoted through sharing of information among actors on their initiatives in this regard.

In recent years, the civil society has played the leading role in the global movement. Civil society organizations were responsible for most of the 75 million signatures on the Manifesto 2000 (see above) during the International Year for the Culture of Peace. And again in 2005, at the midpoint of the United Nations Decade for a Culture of Peace and Non-Violence for the Children of the World, 700 civil society organizations around the world responded to our survey. As described in the website *www.decade-culture-of-peace.org* , most of them reported that they were making progress toward a culture of peace in their own area of work, but that few people knew about it because it was not treated as newsworthy by the mass media or the academic community.

Over the past few centuries, movements of the civil society have had great impact on the world. They are distinguished by lack of hierarchical organization and by the mobilization of mass numbers of people around simple slogans for social change. Among the major social movements have been the abolitionist movement against slavery, the peace movement, disarmament movement, ecology movement, women's movement, labor movement, movements for human rights, democracy movements, indigenous movements and movements for free flow of information. Most recently, many of these movements have found common voice in the World Social Forum.

In recent years, the contributions of social movements to peace have gained recognition through the awarding of the Nobel Peace Prize. In earlier years, the prize often went to men of state power who worked for the end of a particular war, in effect for "negative peace" rather than a culture of peace. Hence, the prize was awarded to such men as Henry Kissinger of the United States, Le Duc Tho of Vietnam, Anwar Al-Sadat of Egypt, Menachem

Begin of Israel, Frederick DeKlerk of South Africa, Yasser Arafat of Palestine, Shimon Peres and Yitzhak Rabin of Israel. It was said that the best way to get the prize was to start a war and then end it. In other cases, however, the prize went to leaders of campaigns for human rights rather than heads of state, including Martin Luther King and Elie Wiesel of the U.S., Adolfo Perez Esquivel of Argentina, Bishop Desmond Tutu of South Africa and Betty Williams and Mairead Corrigan of Northern Ireland. More recently, the prize has gone to the leaders of social movements that contribute in other ways to a culture of peace. These include Joseph Rotblat and Jody Williams (disarmament movements), Aung San Suu Kyi and Shirin Ebadi (democracy and human rights), Wangari Maathai and Al Gore (sustainable development), Muhammad Yunus (economic justice) and Rigoberta Menchu Tum (human rights and indigenous movements). Increasingly, the Nobel Peace Prize has become, in effect, a Nobel Prize for the Culture of Peace.

The closest thing to a coalition of all social movements is the World Social Forum. The Forum has not attempted to develop a formal organizational structure, nor does it issue consensus statements. Instead, it has provided a venue where people can gather and discuss their issues for a week or so every year (beginning in January 2009 it will take place once every two years). Given the fact that Brazil, as we will see later, has taken the lead in the Global Movement for a Culture of Peace at the level of the city, it is not surprising that the World Social Forum was originally a Brazilian city initiative (from Porto Alegre) or that it continues to be coordinated from Brazil. The 2009 Forum took place in Belem, Brazil, with impressive participation by the indigenous peoples of the surrounding Amazon region.. My own experience there, as well as at the 2005 Forum in Porto Alegre, left me with an unforgettable impression of the energy and diversity of participation in social movements around the world.

Let us take a brief look at the history of civil society movements pertaining to the various programme areas of the culture of peace.

Peace and Disarmament movements. A number of years ago, my book *The American Peace Movements,* (Adams 1985) analyzed the major anti-war movements of American history, from the movement against the Spanish-American War at the turn of the 20th Century to the Nuclear Freeze movement of the 1980's. At that time there had been seven movements in the United States that had engaged more than a million people, and since then there has been one more, against the recent war in Iraq. In all cases the movements were reactions against a particular war or threat of war, and their goals could be characterized as a "negative peace", i.e. the end of the particular war in question. In no case did the movement rally around a vision or program for a "positive peace", let alone a "culture of peace." As a result, it was possible for these movements to become very broad, involving people with many different perspectives in which the only common cause was opposition to the war or threat of war at hand.

The recent worldwide peace movement against the War in Iraq has been no exception, also being a reaction against the war rather than a movement for a culture of peace. Thus, for example, although a member of United for Peace and Justice (UFPJ), the main umbrella anti-war organization at the present time in the United States, and although I often put articles about UFPJ onto the website of the Culture of Peace News Network, I have never been asked by UFPJ or its local organizations to speak with them about the culture of peace. The culture of peace is not on their agenda. In fact, the agenda of the peace movement is set by the state, since it is the state that is responsible for the war. As a result, the goals of the peace movement are organized around the central task of lobbying or reforming the state to end the war. In a perverse way, this may help to reinforce the legitimacy of state power.

While traditional peace movements do not provide an institutional framework for the transition to a culture of peace, they do provide a valuable context for consciousness development. For example, although the culture of peace is not on the formal agenda of UFPJ, an Internet search yields 622 references to culture of peace on the UFPJ local events calendar.

Closely related to anti-war movements have been the movements for disarmament. The disarmament movement usually dates its birth to the 1899 conference at The Hague, Netherlands, which sought to limit the use of increasingly destructive weapons in war. In particular the conference called for a ban on bombing from the air, chemical warfare, and hollow point bullets. The conference also established the Permanent Court of Arbitration which later became the International Court of Justice which is still housed in The Hague. The International Peace Bureau, which was instrumental in the 1899 conference, remains active today on behalf of disarmament.

In recent years, the civil society was responsible for the international treaty to ban anti-personnel mines, which was an important breakthrough for which the Nobel Peace Prize (1997) was granted. This is described in the following excerpt from the award presentation by the Nobel prize committee:

"Our warm welcome to you, the representatives of the ICBL, the International Campaign to Ban Landmines, and to you, Jody Williams, the campaign's strongest single driving force. You have not only dared to tackle your task, but also proved that, the impossible is possible. You have helped to rouse public opinion all over the world against the use of an arms technology that strikes quite randomly at the most innocent and most defenceless. And you have opened up the possibility that this wave of opinion can be channelled into political action ..."

"The mobilization of broad popular involvement which we have witnessed bears promise that goes beyond the present issue. It appears to have established a pattern for how to realise political aims at the global level. The ICBL is an umbrella organization for over one thousand nongovernmental organizations, large and small, which have taken up the cause. The Norwegian Nobel Committee wishes to honour them all, and to draw attention to the impact which such broad coordination can achieve."

The hopes for further disarmament after the anti-personnel mine campaign have had very limited success. In the intervening years, the only advance has been the movement against cluster bombs. Meanwhile, the resistance to disarmament by the Great Powers remains as strong as ever. The annual debates on nuclear disarmament at the United Nations are highly politicized and fruitless as the Security Council members (U.S., U.K, France, Russia and China) refuse to renounce or reduce their stockpiles of nuclear weapons and delivery systems. At these debates, a number of non-governmental organizations continue to present their arguments for nuclear disarmament, although their statements get very little publicity in the mass media and, hence, little recognition by the general public.

Ecology movement. Probably the strongest social movement of our era is the ecology movement, which continues to grow as people realize the impact of global warming produced by fossil fuel emissions.

The ecology movement came on the scene in a dramatic fashion at the 1992 United Nations Conference on Environment and Development in Rio de Janeiro, known as the Earth Summit. It attracted the largest number of heads of state ever assembled, as well as the largest gathering ever of non-governmental organizations (NGOs) devoted to ecology. The NGO's issued a statement called the Earth Charter:

> "1. We agree to respect, encourage, protect and restore Earth's ecosystems to ensure biological and cultural diversity.
>
> 2. We recognize our diversity and our common partnership. We respect all cultures and affirm the rights of all peoples to basic environmental needs.
>
> 3. Poverty affects us all. We agree to alter unsustainable patterns of production and consumption to ensure the eradication of poverty and to end the abuse of Earth...
>
> 4. We recognize that national barriers do not generally conform to Earth's ecological realities. National sovereignty does not mean sanctuary

from our collective responsibility to protect and restore Earth's ecosystems...

5 We reject the build up and use of military force and the use of economic pressure as means of resolving conflict. We commit ourselves to pursue genuine peace, which is not merely the absence of war but includes the eradication of poverty, the promotion of social justice and economic, spiritual, cultural and ecological well being.

6. We agree to ensure that decision-making processes and their criteria are clearly defined, transparent, explicit, accessible and equitable.

7. ... those who have expropriated or consumed the majority of Earth's resources or who continue to do so must cease such expropriation or reduce such consumption and must bear the costs of ecological restoration and protection...

8. Women constitute over half of Earth's population. They are a powerful source for change. They contribute more than half the effort to human welfare. Men and women agree that women's status in decision-making and social processes must equitably reflect their contribution...."

I have reproduced here most of the original Earth Charter, as it was reprinted in the monograph *UNESCO and a Culture of Peace* (Adams 1995) because in many ways it foreshadows the culture of peace declaration and programme of action later submitted to the United Nations. It clearly recognizes that the ecological issue is not isolated, but is linked to other aspects of a culture of peace, including non-violence, disarmament, women's equality, democratic participation and free flow of information.

A new Earth Charter, similar in many respects to the original Earth Charter, was later initiated and formalized separately by a group around Maurice Strong who had been the United Nations Under-Secretary General in charge of the Rio Earth Summit. The new version of the Earth Charter retains the broad perspective of the original version and is especially valuable for the development of a culture of peace consciousness. It may be found, as well as the process by which it was developed, on the Earth Charter website at *www.earthcharterinaction.org/about_charter.shtml.*

There are uncounted thousands of ecological initiatives throughout the world, associated with an unprecedented global consciousness of the issues involved. As is typical of social movements, they are distinguished by lack of hierarchical organization and by the mobilization of mass numbers of people around simple slogans. Unlike the case in many other social movements, ecological initiatives have received considerable favorable notice in the mass media as major sectors of the media are themselves convinced of the importance of the ecological message. Of special importance for the present analysis, to be described later, is the International Council for Local Environmental Initiatives.

Movements for human rights, including trade unions. The movement for human rights is an excellent precedent for the Global Movement for a Culture of Peace because it too is based on a normative document of the United Nations, the Universal Declaration of Human Rights (UDHR) adopted by the General Assembly in 1948. The document is all the more remarkable because many diplomats did not agree that human rights should include economic and social rights such as the right to housing, employment and healthcare, and they wanted to confine the Declaration to civil and political rights such as the right to vote and equal protection before the law. However, thanks to the insistence of the socialist states, backed by the newly joining UN members that had gained their freedom from colonialism, and thanks to the remarkable efforts of key diplomats such as Eleonor Roosevelt, the Declaration was expanded to include economic, social and cultural rights. Neverthless, to this day, the United States government has refused to accept these rights and sign the relevant protocols.

The adoption of the UDHR did not immediately yield results, as shown in the following graph:

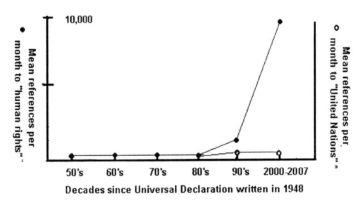

Decades since Universal Declaration written in 1948

* calculated from Social Science Citation Index

The graph shows the citations of human rights in academic publications as monitored by the Science Citation Index. For the first forty years the Declaration was rarely mentioned. It has only in recent years that references have exploded into thousands of times per year.

We may assume that the increased attention to human rights is due largely to the efforts of civil society organizations such as Amnesty International. Amnesty, which won the Nobel Peace Prize (1977), was based on the Universal Declaration of Human Rights. Here is an excerpt from the statement of the Nobel Committee which describes how the organization grew into a worldwide movement:

"The primary aim of Amnesty International is to work to secure the release of people imprisoned for their opinions who have made no use of violence or incited others to do so. These prisoners are called 'prisoners of conscience' ..."

"What, one might ask, are the results of Amnesty International's activities during these last sixteen years? How many prisoners, for example, have been released as a result of Amnesty's efforts? Perhaps the best answer is provided by a single set of statistics covering the period 1972 to 1975, which reveals that of the approximately 6,000 prisoners for whom Amnesty was working at that time 3,000 were released. A great many factors, quite apart from Amnesty, may well have contributed to this result; nevertheless, these figures provide some indication of the scope of the work ...It is still more important to consider Amnesty International's worldwide activities as an integral part in the incessant pressure exerted by all good forces on governments and on the United Nations Organisation, representing a coordinated and necessary effort to achieve an international society founded on justice."

Now almost 60 years after its adoption, the Universal Declaration of Human Rights has been taken up by thousands of other organizations and struggles in all of the other social movements mentioned here as a powerful tool for justice. Hopefully, we will not have to wait so long for such effective use of the Declaration and Programme of Action on a Culture of Peace.

It can be said that the most powerful movement for human rights over the past few centuries has been the trade union movement. Trade unions have fought consistently for such key rights as "a standard of living adequate for the health and well being of himself and of his family, including food, clothing, housing and medical care and necessary social services and the right to security in the event of unemployment, sickness, disability, old age or lack of livelihood in circumstances beyond his control." (Article 25 of the Universal Declaration of Human Rights), as well as the right to work, free choice of employment, and just and favorable conditions of work and protection against unemployment (Article 23) and the right to rest and leisure, including reasonable limitations of working hours and periodic holidays with pay (Article 24).

Because the labor movement threatens the major profits of capitalist exploitation it has been met by the full force of internal military interventions. We have already mentioned the so-called "Industrial Wars" of the 1870's in the United States. Throughout the 20th Century the labor movement has been suppressed frequently by military force in country after country around the world, with the extreme case being that of fascist regimes where the labor movement has often been the first social movement to be brutally crushed.

The labor movement has been weakened in recent years by the flight of industrial enterprises away from the Northern countries where workers have a history of trade union organization and their relocation into poor countries of the South where it has been easier for government-supported capital to suppress trade union organizing. This is an important cause of the growing gap in wealth between rich and poor countries as well as the gap between rich and poor populations within each country.

The labor movement has provided important inputs into other social movements. For example, the great marches of the civil rights movement in the United States associated with Martin Luther King, Jr. were organized by trade union activists. And as shown in my book *The American Peace Movements* (1985), the peace movements attained their greatest strength when the labor movement joined forces with them.

The close relationship between the labor movement and the socialist movement can play a major role in developing alternatives to the culture of war, if it is directed toward strengthening the participation of workers and trade unions in local governance linked with other social movements related to a culture of peace.

Democracy movements. Movements for democracy and national liberation draw their inspiration from the English Revolution at mid 17th Century and the American and French Revolutions at the end of the 18th Century. Another major source of inspiration has come from the national liberation of India by Mahatma Gandhi and his followers, which was accomplished by non-violent means and mass participation of thousands of people on the streets. Their non-violent methodologies have become essential to more recent democracy movements.

Two of the most important democracy movements in recent years have been the successful overthrow of Apartheid in South Africa and the non-violent revolutions to overthrow corrupt governments in the Philippines. The South African and Philippines experiences rank with those of Gandhi in India as models for the development of nonviolent techniques by the civil society which are of essential importance for the transition to a culture of peace. These experiences are described in some detail in the monograph that I wrote for UNESCO (Adams 1995):

The Philippines experience showed the crucial importance of using the latest technological advances in communication, as explained in the following excerpt from the UNESCO monograph:

> "The people of the Philippines in 1986 freed themselves from dictatorship in a process marked by non-violent resistance. During the years of martial law from 1972 to 1986, a movement arose which was characterized by a vast informal network of information, using faxes and photocopies, to expose the true obituaries, movements of the army, information on corruption, etc. At the bottom of each sheet was written 'ipakopiya at ipasa' - copy and pass along. Then, during the elections of 1986 the people came out into the streets by the millions, confronting the tanks and surrounding the radio and television stations to demand the true election results. These results showed that the candidate of the resistance Corazon Aquino had won the vote."

The South African experience showed the great potential of non-violent conflict resolution techniques:

"The Peace Accord was signed by parties which had been locked in combat for a generation: the white majority government and National Party on the one side, and the African National Congress and the Inkatha Freedom Party, on the other. It engaged the entire country in the search for non violent conflict management in a process without any precedent on a national level and which can provide lessons for the rest of the world. ..."

"• National Peace Secretariat. A broad set of regional and local peace committees were established throughout the country, uniting representatives from political organizations, trade unions, business, churches, police and security forces to resolve disputes at local and regional levels. This was the part of the Accord which directly engaged people on a grass roots level throughout the country.

The work of the regional and local peace committees was at the heart of the Accord. It directly engaged people in conflict management on a grass roots level throughout the country. At their peak, there were 11 regional committees and over one hundred local peace committees, with an annual budget of almost $12 million which enabled the hiring of full time staff for regional offices."

Unfortunately, the regional and local peace committees were mostly disbanded after the installation of the new government in South Africa. To retain their function, they would have needed to remain outside the government and there was no source of support for this. Being at UNESCO at that time, I tried to explore possible sources of support through the United Nations, but the bureaucratic obstacles of the UN system could not be overcome.

A recent movement that is often overlooked is the successful non-violent revolution of 1979 by the Iranian people against the Shah and the puppet government that had been established with the help of the Americans and the multi-national oil companies.

Why have the democracy movements not gone further in South Africa, Philippines and Iran? For the same reason that the great revolutions in France, United States, India and Russia ended up producing new imperial powers: they ended up reinforcing the state with its monopoly on the culture of war.

What is needed is a new wave of democracy movements that produce an alternative to state power, an alternative based on the culture of peace at the local and regional levels. In this regard, one of the most promising developments is the practice of participatory budgeting *(presupuesto participativo* in Spanish or *orçamento participativo* in Portuguese) that has been developed in cities in South America and is now spreading around the world. This will be discussed in greater detail below with regard to the experiences of cities and towns for a culture of peace.

Women's movement. Among the most important advances achieved by the civil society have been the gaining of the vote for women and the election of women to parliament and other government positions at all levels from local government to heads of state.

The movement for women's rights has always been linked closely to other aspects of the culture of peace. In the

United States, the movement for women's suffrage originated from the movement to abolish slavery and to the religious "peace sects" such as the Quakers and the evangelical Methodists. One of the first major events of the movement was the convention held in Seneca Falls, New York in 1848, which included among its female participants Elizabeth Cady Stanton and Lucretia Mott, who were experienced abolitionists and the latter a Quaker minister. Also present and speaking at the Seneca Falls Convention was the escaped slave and great abolitionist, Frederick Douglass who later became the close friend and advisor to Abraham Lincoln.   Douglass inspired people with his eloquent and prolific writing, not only against slavery, but also for the rights of women and of organized labor.

Although women have now gained the right to vote in all but a few countries, the women's movement remains active and strong because there is much yet to be accomplished in a constant struggle with gains and losses. During the 1980's in the United States, there was a broad-based movement to amend the Constitution in order to provide equal rights for women, but it was defeated as a result of strong political resistance.   And in recent years, even the rights that American women had previously gained, for example the right to abortion, have been jeopardized by a political and judicial system that has adhered increasingly to a culture of war agenda.   On the other hand, in France, where women did not gain the vote and the right to property ownership regardless of marriage until after World War II, landmark legislation has been adopted in recent years that requires all political parties to put up an equal number of male and female candidates in most elections.

In many, but not all countries, progress has also been made against that extreme form of male domination, rape. Susan Brownmiller's 1975 book, *Against Our Will,* was the product of a powerful movement of women during the 60's and 70's to break the silence surrounding rape. There were thousands of "consciousness-raising groups" of women at that time. As Brownmiller explains, she was inspired by their movement.:

> "I was there when we in the women's movement first began to explore the many aspects of rape, and I listened to those ... who understood the issues far better than I. The movement also made my book possible by its courage and imagination, and by its contribution of personal testimony that opened up the subject of rape from a woman's point of view for the first time in history. Three events deserve specific mention, and I am proud that they were organized by a group to which, I am fond of saying, 'I gave my life's blood.' These were: The New York Radical Feminist Speak-Out on Rape, January 24, 1971; The New York Radical Feminist Conference on Rape, April 17, 1971; and the joint New York Radical Feminist - National Black Feminist Organization Speak-Out on Rape and Sexual Abuse, August 25, 1974."

In peace education there is a strong current of feminists arguing that the struggle against patriarchy is the key struggle for a culture of peace. A particularly effective advocate of this approach is Betty Reardon and her book, *Sexism and the War System* (1985). While there is much to be said for her approach, in my opinion it is only a partial analysis as it does not adequately consider or provide an alternative approach to the culture of war of the state. At one point, however, Reardon's book comes close to the present analysis when it criticizes feminism for its "lack of structural considerations":

> "... women in the third World ... know that all people in their society, both men and women, are oppressed. Although women in these societies are certainly more oppressed, their oppression is part of a total system that such Western feminist analysis has not taken sufficiently into account. Indeed, to assert 'that our oppression is by men and not by opposing nationalities' not only ignores the structures that enforce sexist oppression and contemporary economic paternalism, but also attributes to nation-states a degree of autonomy they simply do not have. This reinforces the myth of sovereignty, which is another significant support of the war system. The assertion also fails to challenge the nation-state itself and all related international structures as essentially patriarchal."

Experience with national culture of peace projects (Lacayo, et al, 1996; Mozambique, 1994) have shown that networks of women in poor, rural and working class neighborhoods are the strongest force for social change based on the principles of a culture of peace. This is consistent with the recognition by all social movements that they need to be closely allied to women's movements and networks to draw strength from women's participation and energy It is understood that no other movement, whether it is peace or labor or ecological sustainability can achieve its goals if women continue to be exploited and treated unfairly.

International understanding, tolerance and solidarity. In fact, it is not possible to single out a particular "movement" for international understanding, tolerance and solidarity because almost all international civil society organizations are involved to one extent or another in this aspect of the culture of peace. Most of the international civil society organizations in the 2005 survey mentioned above are dedicated to this, as well as most of the 475 youth organizations that we surveyed in the follow-up report "Youth for Culture of Peace" (2006) which is available on the same website, *www.decade-culture-of-peace*.org . These reports present a rich source of information on the types of activities being undertaken for international solidarity. Among their activities are:

- *International congresses, symposiums, jamborees, seminars, dialogues, retreats, conferences and workshops*
- *University and summer school courses for international understanding involving international faculty and students*
- *Publication of curricula for international understanding*
- *Publication of pamphlets and books for international understanding*
- *International festivals of culture, cinema and arts*
- *International teacher training courses for culture of peace*
- *International interfaith conferences for inter-religious dialogue*
- *Peace teams and peace missions for direct non-violent intervention in zones of conflict*
- *Caravans, peace tours, and ocean voyages of international solidarity with programmes at the places visited*
- *International youth training programmes for culture of peace skills*
- *International youth solidarity work camps*

- *Internet websites for exchange of perspectives among people, especially children from different parts of the world*
- *Opportunities for travel and study by international students*
- *International encounters of indigenous communities*

Movement for free flow of information. So many journalism professionals have taken up the cause of the free flow of information that one can say it has become a social movement. Perhaps to some extent this is a reaction to increasing monopolization of the mass media by fewer and fewer multi-national corporations with increasingly strong links to the military-industrial complex as noted earlier. Fortunately, the Internet, community radio and small independent newspapers have grown at the same time, providing an outlet for the news that is routinely suppressed by "big media".

An especially effective organization is Reporters Without Frontiers. Their annual report, available from the website at *www.rsf.org*, provides a remarkable compendium of the attacks on reporters and freedom of the press and a strong defense of the freedom of information. Their 2007 report states that "A disturbingly record number of journalists and media workers were killed or thrown in prison around the world in 2006 and we are already concerned about 2007, as six journalists and four media assistants have been killed in January alone. But beyond these figures is the alarming lack of interest (and sometimes even failure) by democratic countries in defending the values they are supposed to incarnate."

Although details are not provided in the press release, the Report does criticize the rich nations of the North as well as the poor nations of the South. For example, it states that "The United States has been largely discredited for its illegal detention of an Al-Jazeera journalist at its Guantanamo military base, by its repeated imprisonment of U.S. journalists for refusing to disclose their sources, the lack of any serious investigation of the deaths of Iraqi journalists shot by U.S. troops and its persistent support for regimes that have no respect for press freedom. The U.S. cannot be trusted when it talks of press freedom."

Although UNESCO supports Reporters Without Frontiers and other such initiatives for freedom of the press, as an inter-governmental organization, the organization has its own limits and taboos. For example, a number of years ago, as Director of the United Nations International Year for the Culture of Peace, I called together a meeting of directors of the physical science sector of UNESCO, the only one of the organization's five sectors that did not support the initiative. I began by asking how their priority, the ethical responsibility of scientists, could be exercised if a scientist had signed an oath of secrecy on his or her work? Even if scientists saw something unethical, they would not be free to discuss it. "And I will wager that at least half of the scientists of the world are working under contractual secrecy, either for the military or for industrial corporations concerned to obtain patents." There was silence, and then one of my favorite colleagues stood and said, "David, I think that is an underestimate!" and he stood up and walked out of the room. The rest followed. The meeting had not lasted more than five minutes. But they waited for me in the corridor outside and congratulated me for breaking the taboo, saying, "We can't talk about that."

In fact, the secrecy of science is a danger to humanity. Who knows what terrible accidents may occur that put life in jeopardy? Is there any truth in the persistent rumors that HIV-AIDS first escaped from a laboratory? And, even if it were not so, what is being done now in biological weapons research and in the extensive experiments with genomes for biomedical purposes that are carried out in secrecy and that could pose future risks to the health of humans, animals and plants?

Whistle-blowers, those who risk their careers and even their lives to make secrets public, are an important part of the movement for a free flow of information. Among the most famous are the American Daniel Ellsberg who made public the Pentagon Papers during the Vietnam War and the Israeli Mordechai Vanunu who revealed secret information about Israel's nuclear weapons, for which he has spent most of his life in prison.

We may expect whistle-blowers to play an increasingly important role in the development of an alternative to state power. As we have seen, the state depends more and more for its power on the control of information. But as the amount of secrecy increases, the number of people with access to secrets, i.e. the number of potential whistle-blowers, also continues to increase. This is one of the weakest points in the culture of war. On the other hand, alternative power should be cultivated on the basis of full transparency that can obtain the confidence of the people and involve them in social change.

The strengths and weaknesses of civil society. Because of its enormous scope and complexity and energy, it is tempting to think that the civil society itself, working independently of the state, and gradually coalescing into a global movement, could eventually bring about a transition from the culture of war to a culture of peace. No doubt, civil society is a powerful force for the culture of peace, and must play a very important role, but for the following reasons, I believe that the civil society cannot do the job alone.

First, civil society organizations are not truly representative of the peoples of the world. Civil society organizations are not elected by the people. Instead, they are self-appointed, and their leadership develops independently within each organization. Of course, they wish to be recognized by the people they serve, and they try as much as possible to involve these people as a force to strengthen and expand their capacities, but, at the same time, they are not required to obtain a mandate from the people. In some cases, they give the people they serve a voice in the decisions about how and what to undertake, but the leadership of the organization itself is not usually chosen by the people at large. This is both a source of strength and a source of weakness. On the one hand, it gives civil society organizations the freedom to be "ahead of their time" and be an educational force for the future. On the other hand, they do not have the democratic legitimacy to become a political counterforce to the culture of war of the nation-state; in the final analysis, the transition from a culture of war to a culture of peace is a question of political power, not just a struggle of ideas and good works.

Second, civil society organizations are often locked in a fierce competition, one against another, for limited resources. For example, many organizations must devote a high proportion of their efforts to finding enough money to pay their staff on an ongoing basis. In doing so, they are competing with other organizations doing the same thing, and the overall effect of the various organizations is greatly reduced.

Third, there is often a lack of synergy among organizations working for different components of the culture of peace. Organizations working in one area, for example, freedom of the press, do not necessarily join forces with organizations working for other areas, for example, disarmament or women's equality. This "fragmentation" of the culture of peace is unlike the unity of the various components of the culture of war.   For example, those working in the arms industry know full well that they are in synergy with those working for economic exploitation, male domination, propaganda for enemy images, and vice versa, those working in these other areas recognize their alliance with the arms industry, etc. The various forces of the culture of war pool their energies in the traditional political process, ensuring that most national presidential campaigns support the various aspects of the culture of war, explicitly or implicitly.

Fourth, much of the energy of civil society is directed toward trying to change policies of the state. No doubt this is important and many important victories have been won, including the prevention of some wars. But in the long run, for the reasons provided earlier, it is not likely that the transition to a culture of peace can be accomplished at the level of the state.   It will be more productive in the future, as will be argued further below, to put more of the energy of the civil society into making changes at the local level, while continuing to think globally.

For all the above reasons, it makes sense to redirect the primary emphasis of the civil society toward working together with elected officials at the local level. That does not mean abandoning completely their national and international work, which will continue to help restrain the culture of war at that level. But it does mean a radical shift of emphasis and priorities if we are to arrive at a culture of peace.

First, by working together with local elected officials the civil society can achieve the legitimacy of working for the people as a whole, and it increases the possibility of broadening the base of involvement to include everyone in he community.

Second, by working together with local elected officials, the civil society can find common ground, above the level of their competition for limited resources. For the projects with city or town officials, resources may be provided by the city or town budget or by foundations and other financial sources that will give their money to a city or town project while they might not give it to a particular non-governmental organization.

Third, by working together on the culture of peace, the civil society organizations that would normally concentrate on their own particular area, can now take part in a more holistic and mutually-reinforcing approach.

Fourth, by putting energy into local government, they can help build the base for a new world order that is free from the culture of war. This is the topic of the following section.

5) THE BASIC AND ESSENTIAL ROLE OF LOCAL GOVERNMENT (CITIES, TOWNS AND LOCAL REGIONS OR PROVINCES) IN CULTIVATING A CULTURE OF PEACE

Over the centuries, as the state has increasingly monopolized the culture of war, the city, town and local region has lost its culture of war, ceding it to the national authorities. If we visit European cities, we can still see fragments of the old city walls with their turrets spaced close enough together for archers or musketeers to shoot an invading enemy on all fronts. In many cases we will see the old gates that could be closed to keep out an invading enemy or to control who could come in and out of the city, much as today's states control the traffic through their customs or douanes at each port of entry into the state.

No longer do cities and towns maintain armies to protect against invasion or to put down internal rebellions. Police forces are armed to encounter one or a few potential "enemies", and one does not imagine them to have tanks, missiles, nuclear weapons and the weapons of the modern battlefield (although there is a problem with their use of automatic weapons). The same is true for the various other areas of the culture of peace in the context of local government. One finds that policies in most of these areas are much less aligned with the culture of war than their equivalents at the national level, and instead one finds considerable evidence of the culture of peace.

Sustainable development is highly developed at the local level. This is reflected in the work of ICLEI, (International Council for Local Environmental Initiatives). ICLEI is a membership association of over 987 local governments, representing over 300 million people worldwide that have made a unique commitment to sustainable development. Their work is based on United Nations decisions, beginning with Agenda 21 that was adopted by the United Nations after the Rio Conference on Environment and Development in 1992. It is described as follows on their website at *www.iclei.org* :

> "Through its international campaigns and programs, ICLEI works with local governments to generate political awareness of key issues; establish plans of action toward defined, concrete, measurable targets; work toward meeting these targets through the implementation of projects; and evaluate local and cumulative progress toward sustainable development.

Our campaigns, programs, and projects promote Local Agenda 21 as a participatory, long-term, strategic planning process that addresses local sustainability while protecting global common goods. Linking local action to internationally agreed upon goals and targets such as Agenda 21, the Rio Conventions, the Habitat Agenda, the Millennium Development Goals and the Johannesburg Plan of Implementation is an essential component.

A fundamental component of our performance-based campaign model is the milestone process. Each campaign incorporates a five-milestone structure that participating local governments work through: (1) establish a baseline; (2) set a target; (3) develop a local action plan; (4) implement the local action plan; and (5) measure results."

Many towns and cities are putting a priority on the development of local, sustainable agriculture, realizing that the increasing globalization of agriculture carries a serious risk of dependence on petroleum and on the global economy. If these should fail, the local community will need to have food resources at its disposal in order to survive. Two examples are the city of Curitiba in Brazil; and Cuba, which, though not a local government, has coped with isolation from the global economy by developing a self-sufficient agricultural system.

Here is an excerpt from the description of Curitiba on ICLEI website:

"Curitiba is referred to as the ecological capital of Brazil, with a network of 28 parks and wooded areas. In 1970, there was less than 1 square meter of green space per person; now there are 52 square meters for each person. Residents planted 1.5 million trees along city streets. Builders get tax breaks if their projects include green space. Flood waters diverted into new lakes in parks solved the problem of dangerous flooding, while also protecting valley floors and riverbanks, acting as a barrier to illegal occupation, and providing aesthetic and recreational value to the thousands of people who use city parks.

The 'green exchange' employment program focuses on social inclusion, benefiting both those in need and the environment. Low-income families living in shantytowns unreachable by truck bring their trash bags to neighborhood centers, where they exchange them for bus tickets and food …Under the 'garbage that's not garbage' program, 70% of the city's trash is recycled by its residents."

The following description of Cuba's ecological initiatives is taken from a longer report by Oxfam America (2001) *Cuba: Going Against the Grain*:

"Cuba has given birth to an ecology-based agriculture. A number of alternative production techniques have been introduced to cope with the lack of chemical inputs and limited fuel, electricity and machinery in food production for domestic consumption. These include organic fertilizer, animal traction, mixed cropping, and biological pest controls. Some have called Cuba, in only a slight overstatement, a national laboratory in organic agriculture.   Cuba's production is also much more diversified, more integrated, and smaller in scale, which leads towards greater sustainability. A major factor in domestic food production has been the explosive growth of urban gardens, which now produce half of the vegetables consumed in Havana, a population of two million people."

Human rights has been measured at the city level by the City of São Paulo (2008) in Brazil, with the methodology and results available on their Internet site. The city's 31 subprefectures are mapped to indicate whether they have high, good, medium or low guarantees of human rights. The measures employed correspond to many of the priorities of every modern city including housing, health care and sanitation, education, and public safety. This is discussed further in the next chapter.

Democratic participation is often more developed at the local level than at the national level. It is sometimes said that this is simply because the scale is smaller, but there are other reasons as well. Cities and towns are relatively free from the enormous influence of the military-industrial complex and the monopoly corporations and financial institutions that weigh so heavily on national policy.

The most important recent advance in democratic participation, participatory budgeting, which began in Latin America (presupuesto particpativo or orçamento participativo) is now spreading to cities and towns throughout the world. The following description of participatory budgeting is drawn primarily from the online page of Wikipedia, and supplemented by other sources.

"Participatory budgeting first developed in the city of Porto Alegre, Brazil, starting in 1989 as a response to severe inequality in living standards, including slum conditions for one third of the city's residents. The process occurs annually, starting with a series of neighborhood, regional, and citywide assemblies, where residents and elected budget delegates identify spending priorities and vote on which priorities to implement.

Porto Alegre spends about 200 million dollars per year on construction and services, and these funds are subject to participatory budgeting. Annual spend on fixed expenses such as debt service and pensions, are not subject to public participation. Around fifty thousand residents of Porto Alegre now take part in the participatory budgeting process (compared to 1.5 million city inhabitants), with the number of participants growing year on year since 1989. Participants are from diverse economic and political backgrounds.

The participatory budgeting cycle starts in January and assemblies across the city facilitate maximum participation and interaction. Each February there is instruction from city specialists in technical and system aspects of city budgeting. In March there are plenary assemblies in each of the city's 16 districts as well as assemblies dealing with such areas as transportation, health, education, sports, and economic development. These large meetings—with participation that can reach over 1,000—elect delegates to represent specific neighborhoods. The mayor and staff attend to respond to citizen concerns. In the following month's delegates meet weekly or biweekly in each district to review technical project criteria and district needs. City department staff may participate according to their area of expertise. At a second regional plenary, regional delegates prioritize the district's demands and elect 42 councillors representing all districts and thematic areas to serve on the Municipal Council of the Budget. The main function of the Municipal Council of the Budget is to reconcile the demands of each district with available resources, and to propose and approve an overall municipal budget. The resulting budget is binding, though the city council can suggest, but not require changes. Only the Mayor may veto the budget, or remand it back to the Municipal Council of the Budget, and this has never yet happened.

The high number of participants, after more than a decade, suggests that participatory budgeting encourages increasing citizen involvement, according to World Bank paper. Also, Porto Alegre's health and education budget increased from 13% (1985) to almost 40% (1996), and the share of the participatory budget in the total budget increased from 17% (1992) to 21% (1999). The paper concludes that participatory budgeting can lead to improved conditions for the poor..."

"Based on the success in Porto Alegre, more than 140 (about 2.5%) of the 5,571 municipalities in Brazil have adopted participatory budgeting. Participatory budgeting has spread to hundreds of Latin American cities, and dozens of cities in Europe, Asia, Africa and North America."

With the defeat of the Workers Party in the Porto Alegre elections in 2004, there appears to have been some regression in adherence by city government to the participatory budgeting process, but according to recent discussion on the website, participatorybudgeting.org, it seems that the process is so well established among the citizenry that they will force the governing party to support it or be defeated in future elections.

As for the **equality of women**, it is certainly more developed in local governance in many countries of the North than it is developed at the national level, thanks to many initiatives at the level of the local communities.   On the other hand, in many countries of the South, such as Cuba, Vietnam, Mozambique, etc., there has been so much progress toward high proportion of women legislators in the national parliament that this sets a precedent to increase the proportion of women in local community governments.

The Federation of Canadian Municipalities (2004) has produced a report entitled A City Tailored to Women: The Role of Municipal Governments in Achieving Gender Equality which is available on the Internet. In addition to providing a questionnaire for assessment of gender equality, the report describes exemplary initiatives from cities in Europe (Berlin, Liège, Barcelona, Amadora-Lisbon, Paris, Prato-Italy, Prague, Saratov-Russia, Stuttgart and Vienna), the Americas (Montreal, San Salvador, Buenos Aires, Santo Andre-Sao Paulo, Cosquin-Argentina, and Quetzaltenango-Guatemala), and Asia (Bangkok, Cebu City-Philippines and Naga-Philippines).

The introduction to the report of the Federation of Canadian Municipalities makes a point that is essential to the argument of the present book: "It has become increasingly clear that action to improve the daily lives of citizens is at its most effective at the local government (municipal) level."

Local communities often have more **solidarity** than at the level of the state, because the essential propaganda of the culture of war, the promotion of enemy images, is much less developed at the local level. Communities may have rivalries, for example, in sports, but these are not enemies to be destroyed in the sense of the culture of war.

Of course, local communities still face problems of intolerance, often involving race, ethnicity and/or religious differences. When communities are located within a state that has a state religion or which engages in the scapegoating or banning of certain groups, it is difficult for the city to escape the consequences. However, one does not usually encounter the reverse situation where there are "city religions" independent of the "state religions" that contribute to a culture of war in some countries. And initiatives for inter-religious and inter-ethnic dialogue are often more successful at the local level than equivalent initiatives at a national or international level.

Transparency and the free flow of information is much more prevalent at the level of the city than at the level of national governments. Perhaps there are some secrets at the level of the city, but nothing like the state secrets of "national security". Transparency is being increased further by new processes such as participatory budgeting mentioned above. With participatory budgeting, not only is the relevant information made available to the citizens, but even more important, the citizens demand to know this information because they must act on its basis in making budgetary decisions.

Education for a culture of peace, which in the past has been considered to be the exclusive business of the schools and universities, is expanding to include the city itself. This is described by Cabezudo (2007, 2008) and is reflected in the very name of the "International Association of Educating Cities" (website at *www.bcn.es/edcities/*). Participatory budgeting is a good example of this as documented in the case of Rosario, Argentina, by Lerner and Schugurensky (2005).. Here are key excerpts from their conclusion, which is available on the Internet:

> "Rosario residents who regularly engaged in participatory budgeting experienced significant learning in a wide variety of fields. [They] became more familiar with the needs of different communities, got to know new and different people, and acquired instrumental and technical knowledge about politics and citizenship. This knowledge can allow them to better represent their communities, develop political efficacy, establish networks and partnerships with other groups, and develop solidarity with people that are worse off. Delegates also developed a variety of instrumental, analytical, leadership, and deliberative skills. Participation nurtured new attitudes, values, and dispositions, especially self-confidence, concern for the common good and public property, tolerance and patience, solidarity, feelings of belonging and connection, and interest in community participation. Finally, delegates changed their daily practices, increasing the level, range, and quality of their civic involvement by becoming more active in the community, diversifying their everyday activities, and adopting more democratic behaviors…"

> "Our data suggests that participatory democracy indeed makes better citizens, if we consider more knowledgeable, skilled, democratic, engaged, and caring citizens to be better citizens.

The findings confirm that participatory budgeting provides a powerful learning experience, and help us better understand what people learn through participation. Neighborhood and district assemblies, training and information sessions for budget delegates, regular work meetings of delegates and community members, consultations between delegates and city staff, and neighborhood tours all function as educative spaces. The extensive learning and changes expressed by the delegates who participated in these activities in Rosario not only validate participatory budgeting's status as a "school of citizenship," but also indicate what participants learn and how they change through this school..."

The use of peaceful conflict resolution and mediation in schools was the subject of an international survey that we undertook at UNESCO in 1996. For the survey we engaged the International Center for Cooperation and Conflict Resolution at Columbia University, under the direction of Professor Morton Deutsch. Their unpublished study, which was to be the basis of a project in schools coordinated by UNESCO, found that there were already thousands of such initiatives in existence by 1996:

"Judging from the early results, school based programmes of conflict resolution are most developed in the United Sates and Canada, where, in response to a significant increase in violence among youth, there was a rapid upsurge in the last decade. There are a number of high quality training Centres and several thousand school programmes. A similar upsurge now appears to be starting for similar reasons in other areas of the world. In Europe a number of

Centres have emerged recently and in 1990 a European Network for Conflict Resolution in Education was formed.   In Australia and in Israel there are a number of well-developed Centres and school programmes. Little data was forthcoming, however, for Latin America and the Caribbean, Asia and the Pacific, Arab States and Africa, with the exception of South Africa where there are several very active conflict resolution centres. The report includes full case studies of eight programmes from Australia, Japan, US, Northern Ireland, South Africa, Israel, Norway and France."

Although the UNESCO project was never established due to bureaucratic obstacles, there was an international meeting in Sintra, Portugal, which issued a remarkable statement on the need for such an approach. See the Sintra Plan of Action available on the Internet at UNESCO (1996).

Security and public safety is a concern in every community as urban violence has attained epidemic proportions in many cities of the world. This is reviewed in the report, *Human Security for an Urban Century: Local Challenges, Global Perspectives* which has been issued by the Human Security Policy Division at Foreign Affairs and International Trade Canada (2007), available on the Internet. Among the chief concerns are *homicide rates* and *number of police per capita*. The latter must be qualified by another suggested indicator which is that of *corruption*, since police do not make a city more secure if they are corrupt!   The human security report indicates that public safety is closely related to other aspects of a culture of peace such as *perceived access to decision-making* and *participation in community organizations* (democratic participation) and *percentage of population in slums, land tenure,* and *access to public services* (human rights). The indicator of *homicide* *rates* may be related to other important issues which include rates of other types of crimes and rates of gun ownership (especially automatic weapons) and measures of gun control. The report notes, for example, that in Brazil, more than 100 people are killed by firearms every day, and that banning the carrying of guns in Bogotá during traditionally violent holidays or late at night has been shown to reduce rates of violence.

It is not the thesis of this book that cities and towns, no matter how effective their policies, can create a culture of peace by themselves. Instead, however, experience with **some ongoing initiatives** shows that they can be the basis for a new culture of peace with the collaboration of civil society, on the one hand, and a global network of local governments, on the other hand. Looking back at the previous chapter we can see the following advantages deriving from the linkage of local government with civil society:

As described above in the consideration of civil society, an essential contribution can be made by local governments by providing:

1) democratic legitimacy and the involvement of the entire community in the work of the civil society;

2) a venue where the civil society can cooperate without needing to compete for limited resources;

3) a venue where the civil society organizations promoting the various aspects of a culture of peace can cooperate in a holistic and mutually-reinforcing way; and

4) the basis for a new world order that is free from the culture of war.

At the same time, when working with local government the civil society makes essential contributions to a culture of peace that could not otherwise be done by local government working alone:

1) passion, energy and local experience in each of the various areas of a culture of peace

2) linkage to global movements concerned with each of the various areas of a culture of peace

3) continuity when local government changes hands in election reversals

To put the culture of peace into practice at a local level, culture of peace commissions have been established in Brazilian cities and provinces. By the end of 2007, commissions had been established in the cities of São Paulo, Itepecirica da Serra, São José dos Caompos and Diadema, all within the State of São Paulo, and Curitiba and Londrina in the State of Parana. Two other cities were in the process of establishing such commissions in Ribeirão Pires and Cotia. And they follow the establishment earlier of a Culture of Peace Council in the Legislative Assembly of the State of São Paulo, thanks to the inspired leadership of Lia Diskin and her organization, Palas Athena. Also, as mentioned above, São Paulo has pioneered in the measurement of human rights at the city level.

Cities in North America and Europe are in the process of establishing similar commissions at the end of 2008. This includes Hamilton (Ontario) in Canada and New Haven (Connecticut) in the United States where a city peace commission, previously engaged for the most part with national and international issues, is now considering work on the culture of peace at a local level.

The commissions in Brazil and North America are composed of both legislators and representatives of civil society organizations. In this way, they integrate the initiatives and perspectives of government and civil society. For example, the Culture of Peace Council of the Legislative Assembly of the State of São Paulo has six elected deputies from the three main political parties and 35 representatives from civil society organizations working in all of the various areas of the culture of peace. As one of its recent actions, the Commission has distributed widely a guidebook on the work for culture of peace by the various civil society organizations involved.

Because the culture of peace integrates a broad range of program areas, including not only disarmament, but also peace education, equality of women, human rights, tolerance and solidarity, democratic participation, free flow of information and sustainable development, it provides a platform to integrate different departments of government. For example, a recent event in São Paulo was sponsored by the secretariats for human rights and for the environment, and brought together government workers in health, social work, education and police as well as civil society organizations in all these areas.

The initial Culture of Peace Council, at the level of the State of São Paulo, came about in conjunction with the campaign of the International Year for the Culture of Peace, under our leadership at UNESCO in 2000, to obtain commitments on the Manifesto 2000, as described above. The process by which this first Culture of Peace Council was founded is described on the website of the Comitê Paulista para a Década da Cultura de Paz (2001-2010).

In Hamilton, Ontario, the initiative for a Culture of Peace Commission has much in common with the initiative in São Paulo. It also is led by the civil society organizations that came together in 2000 around the campaign for the International Year for the Culture of Peace and the dissemination of the Manifesto 2000. It also is going through the process of gaining official status from the Mayor and the City Council. Our presentation to the City Council in October 2008 followed discussions about garbage cans and dog-parks, putting peace at the level of day-to-day life for ordinary citizens.

Some flavor of the work of the São Paulo Council can be obtained from the cycle of six conferences it sponsored in 2007 for "multipliers" by specialists in strategic tools for culture of peace building. "It is an honor to be here with those who are working to build a Culture of Peace", said José Gregori, President of the São Paulo Human Rights Committee, ex-Foreign Affairs Minister, when he opened the first conference on March 21. Sixty persons, including deputies, leaders of NGOs, journalists, lawyers, civil servants of the legislative branch, and parliament representatives attended. Other conferences concerned ethics in public life, democracy, power, and the legislative process, restorative justice and public policies, complexity in public policies, and Gandhi, a serving leader.

Several of us have been working with the various City Commission initiatives to establish an annual assessment of the culture of peace, with locally-developed indicators for each of the programme areas of the culture of peace. By making the same measurements every year, it should be possible help city government know which policies are working and in what areas they need to improve their policies. And by involving people from the community to make the culture of peace measurements related to their work (teachers, journalists, women activists, religious leaders, trade unionists, police, etc.), this can broaden the base of culture of peace work and serve as an educational process. More about this in the following chapter.

6) ASSESSING PROGRESS TOWARD A CULTURE OF PEACE AT THE LOCAL LEVEL

My scientific training leads me to believe that it is essential to measure progress toward a culture of peace at the local level. But it should not be reduced to a simple formula, or calling in "experts" to do the job. Instead, it needs to be a process of regular assessment to know if the initiatives we take are successful or not, what works and what doesn't work, and whether we are making progress.

The process of assessment, to be consistent with the basic principles of a culture of peace, needs to be participatory and educational. The people who are concerned with the various areas of a culture of peace need to be those who are engaged in the process of assessment, and they need to be engaged in a participatory way, so that they take part in the decision-making of how, what, and when to make the assessments. In other words it should be "self-assessment" rather than "outside-assessment". And the entire process should be designed to be educational, so that those who take part are constantly learning as they go forward, and constantly teaching those with whom they come into contact. In fact, this reflects the fundamental nature of culture itself which is a process that involves the entire society and in which everyone is constantly learning and teaching at the same time. As the original UNESCO document, Co-operation to promote a culture of peace (140EX/28), stated in 1992: "the guiding principle would be that each person has something to learn from everyone else, and has something to give in return."

The use of indices for a culture of peace should never be used to "prove" that one entity (country, city or civil society organization) is better than another. An especially bad example of this kind of misuse of indices is the use of testing scores to compare schools. This has become national policy in the United States and Canada with disastrous results. Schools and teachers are required to compete for funding, which leads to widespread cheating and a loss of confidence in the entire system of education.

Instead of comparing one organization to another, indices are useful to indicate whether the local situation is improving from year to year, and which areas of the index are improving or regressing. This is comparable to stock exchange indices; they are useful not for absolute comparisons between one stock exchange and another, but rather to show trends within a particular stock exchange and within each sector of stocks in a particular exchange.

Another useful result will be new ideas for initiatives to address weaknesses that emerge during the process of assessing the policies and programmes that are already in place. In fact, the forward-looking proposals may turn out to be even more important than the backward-looking assessments.

At the level of the town or city, the annual assessment of a culture of peace index can be an important central task for a culture of peace commission. In keeping with the above analysis, the index should be different for each town or city, reflecting its own particular cultural context and allowing the people of that community to be involved in the measurement process and the development of new initiatives.

The assessment should be based on the programme areas identified by the United Nations Declaration and

Programme of Action on a Culture of Peace.   This is the only way to attain universally valid results in a subject which otherwise would be politicized and controversial.   Seven of the programme areas in the UN document can be applied directly to the municipal level as well as at the national level. The eighth area, international peace and security, does not apply directly and therefore it may be applied as two separate programme areas: 8) security, i.e. public safety; and 9) solidarity with other municipalities on an international level.

It is important that the index initiative be an occasion for outreach and involvement of new people that are not already on the commission or in the city government. This not only ensures that there is no conflict of interest in the process, but it also helps to mobilize and educate new constituencies of the culture of peace. In the long run, this mobilization and education is essential to progress toward a culture of peace. Here are some examples of constituencies that can be engaged:

> * For the assessment of education for a culture of peace: teachers, school board members and administrators, and students themselves, etc.

> * For the assessment of security and disarmament: police, police monitoring boards, community groups that have been formed in response to violence, etc.

> * For the assessment of the free flow of information: journalists from both mainstream and alternative media, citizen groups for access to information, etc.

> * For the measurement of democratic participation: activists from both mainstream

and alternative political parties, neighborhood betterment organizations, electoral commissions, etc.

* For the assessment of women's equality: women activists from all kinds of organizations, neighborhoods, ethnic groups, etc.

* For the assessment of sustainable development: activists from ecological and environmental organizations, city commissions dealing with development, Chambers of Commerce, local agricultural and farmers markets initiatives, etc.

* for the assessment of human rights, a mix of organizations, including trade unions, that defend the rights of workers, children, women, handicapped, poor people, older people, immigrants, indigenous peoples, racial minorities, etc.

* for the assessment of understanding, tolerance and solidarity, those working for inter-religious and/or inter-ethnic dialogue, traditional peace movement activists who work against the labeling of enemies, etc.

Here is one way that a session might proceed with a group assessing one of the programmes area:

1) Think of the most important policies and programmes addressing this area in the preceding one to five years, and how effective they have been.

2) Can their effectiveness be measured separately for each of the various neighborhoods of the city?

3) Next think of the most important policies and programmes in this programme area that you would like to see in the future.

4) Break this down into short-term and long-term perspectives:

   a) policies and programmes that could be instituted in the next few years and how they could be evaluated, if possible, by neighborhood.

   b) policies and programmes that could be instituted in the next 20 years and how they could be evaluated and, if possible by neighborhood.

A score resulting from this approach is especially designed for long-term assessment. It does not start at zero, because it assumes some progress has been made. Also the index will not be at maximum, because progress has not yet been achieved on the future objectives, and it will not reach its maximum in a few years, because some of the objectives are long-term.

The process of measuring a culture of peace should be an educational experience for all who are involved in it. It is an example of "educating cities." This is similar to the findings mentioned above concerning participation in another city-wide process, the participatory budgeting process that has been so effective in South America. Just as the citizens involved in participatory budgeting learn how a city works and how its budget process works, so, too, citizens involved in measuring a culture of peace will come to learn what the culture of peace is all about. The learning process in each case goes beyond those making the assessment: City administrators learn from citizen participation; and all those involved with the culture of peace will learn from the citizens who take part in its measurement. Finally, the general public can learn from media presentations of the process.

In order to reflect the holistic quality of the culture of peace, the overall index in any particular town or city should be the sum of sub-indices, one for each of the programme areas of a culture of peace, and each of the sub-indices should be given equal weight, since they are all important.   At first glance, this might not seem very important, but since the entire exercise is in part a process of education, one needs to respect the holistic quality of the culture of peace.

By measuring all of the programme areas for the culture of peace each year, it can be seen whether particular policies are succeeding, and it should be possible to find weaknesses and unmet needs and to propose new policies and programmes to address them.   In other words, the culture of peace index can help the municipal authorities to make policy decisions.   There are several guidelines that flow from this:

> First, it is important that the index and sub-indices should be real numbers, either quantitative measures or quantitative representations of qualitative assessments. Otherwise, it will not be possible to make comparisons from one year to another and to know whether the assessment index and sub-indices are improving or regressing.

Second, the index and sub-indices should include both short-term and long-term measures. Short-term measures should be included to that the index can accurately reflect policy decisions from one year to another and to know if they are effective. Long-term measures should be included so that the index can show progress over many years and decades. After all, it took the culture of war 5,000 years to reach its full maturity, and we can expect the culture of peace to take many centuries to mature.

Third, they should be easy to measure, i.e. they should involve measurements that are not so time-consuming and/or expensive that they cannot be done every year.

Fourth, they should be appropriate for the town, city or province concerned. This can only be determined by people from that community who are engaged by the culture of peace commission to measure a particular programme area. And this means that each community will have a unique measure that cannot be directly compared to that of other communities, and only compared to itself from one year to another in order to see trends. No doubt, it will be useful for those involved in the process to look at the methods used by other cities, some of which are mentioned below. However, they should not simply copy the methods used in other cities and towns but should develop a unique measure appropriate to their own community.

Fifth, it will be useful if the index and sub-indexes can be measured in the same way across the many administrative subdivisions of the community, especially in the case of large cities. In each community this may vary; for example, it could be measured by election districts, administrative districts or school districts. This will be very useful for evaluation of policies and establishing future priorities. There is, of course, the danger that this could be mis-used as we have discussed above concerning school testing. Since this kind of mis-use of statistics contradicts the basic principles of a culture of peace, one of the tasks of a culture of peace commission is to guard against this danger and prevent its occurrence.

Once the process of measuring the culture of peace has been established and carried out over a few years, it should prove to have other very important uses. For example:

* A culture of peace index can be used in advertising for tourism. Tourism, in fact, is the largest non-agricultural industry in the world, when you include airlines, hotels, etc.. "Come to our city and see a culture of peace in action!" can be an effective advertising slogan. Peace is very attractive for tourists. First of all, its opposite, violent conflict, is the most powerful obstacle to tourism: no one wishes to be a tourist where there is the threat of being the victim of violence. And second, since a culture of peace is informative, it means that the city can offer the tourist a learning experience.

* A culture of peace index can be very well integrated into the practice of "twinning" with cities or towns in other parts of the world. Twinned cities can exchange their experiences

with measuring a culture of peace and adopting policies to strengthen the culture of peace in the community.

* A culture of peace index will focus attention on important tasks that might otherwise escape notice. For example, by taking seriously the possibility of the crash of the culture of war, it can initiate planning for local food production as discussed further in the following chapters.

* Work for a culture of peace will provide a common task with other towns and cities around the world that are also assessing their culture of peace, and will make possible a new level of international solidarity that is not mediated by the state.

Specific indicators have been used by cities to measure each of the programme areas of a culture of peace. Here are some examples.

Sustainable development. The questionnaire of ICLEI (International Council for Local Environmental Initiatives) addresses many issues that can be used as the basis for indicators of sustainable development. Here are some of the highlights :

"* Is there a municipal council decision for a local sustainable development process or plan, and, if so, what resources have been made available (dedicated staff, time from other staff, budget allocation, in-kind support) and over what time period?

* What other stakeholder organizations have been involved and to what extent (business

associations, small to medium enterprises, large companies/industry, job recruitment agencies, trade unions, community groups working with particular constituencies, religious and other non-governmental organizations, environmental organizations, municipal departments of public services, utilities, etc., schools and universities, etc.)

* Does the local authority provide training (and if so, how much) on sustainable development issues to: councilors? senior staff? other staff? stakeholders?

* Does the local authority raise awareness of sustainable development issues in the community (if so, how much) through: local media? newsletters? leaflets? websites? public lectures? open days? exhibitions and festivals? events with specific target groups such as schools or business? Creative approaches such as arts and theatre?

* How many of the following issues are addressed in your local government process/plan for sustainable development: local economy? green business? social economy? employment? social cohesion? health & safety? natural resources? energy? waste & pollution? fair trade? sustainable lifestyles, global climate protection? public and alternative transportation? land use? urban management tools?" [editor's note: I would add here another important issue which is local agricultural development and markets, including organic farming]

"* Has measurable progress been achieved in terms of policy and/or tangible results in the preceding list of issues?

* To what extent is the local authority networking with other local authorities on local sustainable development issues?"

Human rights. As mentioned earlier, the City of São Paulo (2008) has measured human rights in the 31 sub-prefectures of that city for the years 2004, 2005 and 2006. General socio-economic indicators included income levels, sewer access, literacy, housing, employment and infant mortality. Violence indicators included homicide, assault and deaths by police action, Indicators for children and youth included levels of education, hospitalization for acute respiratory infection, illegal acts and institutionalization for aggression. Indicators for women included comparisons with men for level of unemployment and income, votes for female candidates for city council, and rates of abortion, teenage pregnancy, death in childbirth, and access to prenatal care. Indicators for Blacks were, for the most part, similar to those for women: comparisons with whites for level of unemployment and income, rates of teenage pregnancy and access to prenatal care, as well as a comparison of homicide rates of Blacks and whites.

The maps of São Paulo, according to the human rights measures, provide a remarkable picture of the progress towards human rights in that city. Over the three years measured, there has been a measurable progress: in 2004 only three subprefectures had high levels of human rights while six were precarious. By 2006, the situation had reversed and seven had high levels while only two were precarious. The São Paulo data have policy implications. They identify the neighborhoods where the city needs to concentrate its efforts regarding each of the various aspects of human rights. In this regard, each subprefecture has its strong points and its weak points. No subprefecture has a high rating in all five components. For example, while Aricanduva, Vila Mariana, Pinheiros, Sé, Lapa, Butanta and Santana/Tucuruvi are high in the socioeconomic rights, they are all low on the dimension of Negro rights, where instead the highest scores are those of Campo limpo Cap. Socorro, Cidade Ademar, Cidade Tiradentes, Guainases, M'Boi Mirim and São Mateus.

Democratic participation. The International Observatory on Participatory Democracy (2006) has produced a methodology for evaluating participatory democracy which is available on the Internet. In addition to participatory budgeting, it provides suggestions for the evaluation of other municipal processes such as the preparation of strategic municipal plans, local economic development, sustainability, and education projects.

Although it does not provide specific quantitative indicators, the OIDP methodology does provide general principles for evaluation of specific initiatives and processes, which include the following: consensus, initiative and leadership; integration in the municipal system, clarity of objectives, planning and resources, number and diversity of participants in initiatives, openness of the process, relevance to people's lives, level of participation including capacity to make proposals, quality of information provided, results implementation and feedback, improvement of relationships among participants, and training. For details, see their website (International Observatory on Participatory Democracy, 2006).

Women's equality. A specific list of indicators for women's equality has been published by the Federation of Canadian Municipalities, as mentioned earlier. Here are some of the gender-specific items. The full list is available on the Internet (Federation of Canadian Municipalities, 2004).

Affirmative action policies in municipal political parties and parity in committees, commissions and para-municipal enterprises

Network of elected women representatives

Council-adopted policy on gender equality developed through public consultation and carried out via annual municipal plan of action

Public consultation policies with mechanisms to encourage women's participation

Policies and commitments to fight violence against women and increase their safety

Gender perspective in all programs including annual municipal budget and sectoral budgets

Annual gender equality action plan with specific goals, indicators, budget as well as access to gender-disaggregated data on all urban issues and gender impact assessment of urban policies, programs and service delivery

Training in gender mainstreaming for elected officials and staff, men and women

Equal opportunity program for hiring with specific targets for different types of jobs

Women's advisory council, commission or committee within council to monitor implementation of gender equality policy as well as women's advisory councils in the boroughs, neighborhoods or districts

Tolerance and solidarity. Faced with serious problems of tensions between different populations, including minorities and immigrants, the Council of Europe has undertaken the task of measuring social cohesion with an extensive array of questions and indicators. The list of questions is too long to summarize here. Even if one combines the separate sections for minorities and immigrants, there remain over 200 questions, most of which concern differences in the conditions of life between these groups and the general population. For details, see Council of Europe (2005).

Transparency. The Spanish organization, Transparency International España has taken the lead in evaluating transparency at the municipal level. Their publication, "Indice de Transparencia de los Ayuntamientos 2008," measures transparency in 100 Spanish municipalities.

Among the kinds of information covered by the Spanish indicators are the various municipal offices and functions, all agendas, decisions, acts, agreements, decrees and regulations of the city council or its equivalent, rules and regulations for citizen participation, and extensive information on accounting and finances for all city planning and public works, bidding procedures, contracts, etc. A special emphasis is put on making extensive information about these and related matters available to the public via the Internet. For details, see the Website of Transparency International España (2008).

Peace education. Although it has not been possible to find a specific questionnaires for peace education in cities, questions can be based on the recommendations on formal, non-formal and informal education from the UNESCO report to the United Nations Secretary-General on the culture of peace (United Nations 2000).

Formal education proposals in the UNESCO report include training of education personnel at all levels in the content, learning methods and skills needed to promote peace and non-violence and revision of existing and creation of new curriculum materials, and particularly of history textbooks, to promote mutual understanding and strengthen social cohesion and to remove prejudices or stereotypes against certain groups; It also proposes that the culture of peace should be modeled in the policies and practices of the classroom, the school and other learning environments, providing opportunities for all members of the school community to participate in democratic decision-making and governance processes.

Although not mentioned as such in the UNESCO report, it is important to measure the extent to which girl children receive equal educational opportunities as boy children, as well as the comparative educational opportunities for minorities and immigrants, including opportunities for education in their own language.

Non-formal education proposals include the development of methods of peaceful conflict resolution and non-violence. This should include traditional conflict resolution approaches and methods that take into consideration the current political climate, as well as new information technologies. It is also proposed to strengthen the active role of the family and the local community in a participatory approach to determining what a culture of peace means, and how it can be promoted in the local context;

Informal education proposals address the promotion of culture of peace values by sports, dance, theatre and other athletic and artistic activities involving children and youth, the press, television, cinema, video games and the Internet, including not only films but also cartoons, comics, even news programmes available to children and youth. Media education and monitoring and maintaining collective consumer pressure on those who produce and distribute mass media by parents associations, community organization, consumer organizations and institutions are proposed in order to promote the values of a culture of peace, and freedom from the promotion of violence, intolerance, racism and sexual exploitation.

Security. At least two sets of security indicators are available on the Internet. One is a set of indicators developed at Georgetown University in the US and applied to cities in Brazil. The other set has been used for measuring public security in Boston. Here is a combined synopsis. Indicators marked with an asterisk should be measured separately for adult and juvenile offenders. For details, see Georgetown University Political Database of the Americas (2007) and Boston Indicators Project (2008).

Rate of homicides*
Rate of robberies*
Rate of injuries from weapons*
Thefts*
Rate of suicides*
Intra-family violence
Sexual crimes*
Number of complaints filed*
Weapons violations (violations of laws or ordinances prohibiting the manufacture, sale, purchase, transportation, possession, concealment or use of firearms)*
Hate crimes*
Load of system of justice
Level of victimization

Perception of insecurity
Number of police
Number of private security guards
Number of guns per capita
Number of handguns per capita
Number of automatic weapons per capita

Inter-relationships among the various measures. In distinguishing the various programme areas, it is important not to lose sight of the fact that they are all inter-related to a general overall culture of peace. Here are some examples of this inter-relationship:

The *human rights* assessment of Sao Paulo includes measurements of personal violence such as homicide and assault *(security)* and measures of *women's equality* in economics, politics and physical health.

Democratic participation, as assessed by the International Observatory on Participatory Democracy includes measures of *sustainable development, education,* and *access to information.*

The assessment of *sustainable development* by the International Council for Local Environmental Initiatives includes measures of the involvement of *women* and *ethnic minorities,* as well as *stakeholder participation* and *education.*

Equality of women, as assessed by the Federation of Canadian Municipalities, includes measures of *political participation,* prevention of violence against women *(security)* and access to *information.*

The Spanish initiative of transparency *(free flow of information)* puts a high priority on information concerning opportunities for *democratic participation,* including information about municipal decisions so that voters can make informed choices.

The Council of Europe measurement of social cohesion of minorities and immigrants *(understanding, tolerance and solidarity)* includes measures of *women's equality*, access to *education*, including in minority languages, and access to *information* and *democratic participation*, as well as many general *security* and *human rights* issues.

Assessment of *security* in Sao Paulo and Boston includes measures of sexual crimes *(women's equality)* and hate crimes *(tolerance and solidarity)*.

Education for peace, as conceived in the UNESCO report, emphasizes freedom from the promotion of violence *(security)*, intolerance and racism *(understanding, tolerance and solidarity)* and sexual exploitation *(women's equality)* in the various sources of informal education. It also demands that the classroom and school should be a model for culture of peace, including *participation in democratic decision-making and governance.*

Culture of Peace measurement at the level of the state. Consistent with our analysis of the state in this book, the attempts to measure progress toward a culture of peace at the level of the state have been disastrous. They have not been participatory, and, because of the nature of the state, it is difficult to imagine how they could be.

A first attempt was made by a Korean team in 2000 and published under the title, World Culture of Peace Index (2000). On the basis of the criteria they chose, the top countries were those of Scandinavia, while the bottom countries were those of Africa and Asia. The major powers,

England, France, Germany, China, USA, Canada, Australia, Japan, Korea, came out in the middle.

A subsequent article on national indicators for a culture of peace in the Journal of Peace Research by DeRivera (2004) came out with similar rankings, although fewer countries were chosen for study. But this article went further and claimed on the basis of its failure to find a single culture of peace factor, that the culture of peace might be a "flawed concept." In my opinion, it is a kind of sophistry to analyze culture of peace as the quality of existing states, negate it by means of factor analysis, and then declare that the culture of peace concept is "simplistic." As we have argued here, a culture of peace and non-violence, understood in the sense of the original UNESCO proposal as a hypothetical alternative to the culture of war and violence, does not exist at the level of the nation-state.

We should be skeptical of any national indicators that show the nations of the north as peaceful and those of the south as less peaceful. This, too, is a kind of sophistry and hypocrisy. For example, as pointed out by Member States from the South in the 1999 UNESCO debate, notes of which are available on my website at *www.culture-of-peace.info/annexes/commissionV/summary.html* , the states that cry loudest for human rights and "free" elections are at the same time the major sellers of armaments and traditional opponents of independent media in poor countries. This kind of hypocrisy was criticized by African ambassadors, Nouréini Tidjani-Serpos of Benin and Bakary Tio-Touré of Cote d'Ivoire among others, when we held meetings at UNESCO with the Member States by region in March 1998. They stated that one should not look to the South for the causes of the culture of war, and they posed three questions. From where do the weapons come? From where do the violent television programmes come? And where are the terms of trade decided that impoverish the people of the South which leads to violence?"

More recently, one sees again the hypocrisy of measuring peace by nation-state indicators, as exemplified by the new Global Peace Index (2007). How convenient that Europe, Japan, Australia and Canada come out as the most peaceful, while the countries of the South come out as less peaceful! If one needs evidence for the existence of "cultural imperialism", here it is!

7) GOING GLOBAL: NETWORKING OF LOCAL CULTURE OF PEACE COMMISSIONS

Once culture of peace commissions have been established in cities and towns, the next step should be linking up with commissions in other communities and in other parts of the world. This will strengthen the process at the local level though the sharing of best practices and resources, including North-South linkages. It will also develop the basis for a new world order that is based on the culture of peace instead of the culture of war.

At the present time, the most appropriate mechanism for global linkage is the United Cities and Local Governments, which was founded in 2004 as a merger of United Towns Organisation, the International Union of Local Authorities, and Metropolis. The UCLG represents most of the national and regional local government associations throughout the world, which, in turn, represent most local governments in 112 countries. In the fall of 2007, I was pleased to participate in a meeting that they organized in Barcelona about the role of cities in peace-building. A main thrust of the meeting concerned solidarity actions by cities in the North with cities engaged in post-conflict peace-building in the South, and interest was also expressed in promoting a culture of peace within participating cities. As a follow-up in 2009, we are hoping to conclude an agreement between the Fundación Cultura de Paz, the Diputacio of Barcelona (the Barcelona region), and the City Diplomacy Commission of UCLG to develop indicators for the assessment of culture of peace in participating cities.

Networking should also be done along the lines of the various programme areas of the culture of peace. We have already mentioned several global networks of city initiatives that concentrate on individual programme areas that are part of a culture of peace. These include:

> * International Council for Local Environmental Initiatives (ICLEI at *www.iclei.org*)

> * The International Observatory on Participatory Democracy (OIDP) at *www.oidp.net/*

> * International Association of Educating Cities at *www.bcn.es/edcities/*

> * Mayors for Peace at *www.mayorsforpeace.org/english/index.html*

The advantages of global networking of local government culture of peace initiatives are many, including:

> * Sharing of information, including best practices and innovative ideas

> * Mutual inspiration and encouragement

* Increased visibility through partnerships and by attention from the mass media and academic researchers, as well as the potential for Internet site(s) devoted to local government culture of peace initiatives

* Linkages not only with other local governments, but also with the civil society initiatives that are engaged with them

* Opportunities for direct contacts through regional and international conferences and through pairing arrangements

* Eventual development of an international political force for the culture of peace that is independent of the nation-state (see next section)

8) THE FUTURE TRANSITION OF THE UNITED NATIONS FROM CONTROL BY STATES TO POPULAR CONTROL THROUGH LOCAL GOVERNMENTAL REPRESENTATIVES

My experience working in the United Nations system for ten years and observing it closely for seven years since my retirement makes me optimistic that the UN system is capable of managing a transition to the culture of peace. The various specialized agencies that deal with health care, education, food and agriculture, science, communication, not to mention technical questions such as aviation, shipping, atomic energy, etc. are staffed by a capable international secretariat with experience in the day-to-day management of global issues. The UN General Assembly, as well as the international assemblies of other agencies such as the General Conference of UNESCO, provide important forums.

Even the Security Council, the World Bank and the International Monetary Fund which are now in the hands of a few powerful states and used to support their culture of war could play important roles in the transition to a culture of peace if they were transformed under control of "we the peoples" instead of the state.

For the reasons given throughout this book, a global network of local authorities is the best chance for an international political force independent of the nation-state that could take responsibility for the United Nations and direct it towards a culture of peace.

The United Nations system as it is presently constituted must follow the directions of the Member States, and at the present time, those directions help the Member States maintain the culture of war. This became clear when I was helping develop UNESCO Culture of Peace Programme in the 1990's. We were able to develop proposals for national culture of peace programmes in El Salvador and Mozambique involving government agencies and civil societies from both sides of the previous conflict to work together after the signing of their peace accords. The El Salvador programme (Lacayo et al 1996) is described in an academic article and the Mozambique programme (Mozambique 1994) is described in a detailed funding proposal. Both of these are available on the Internet.

The national culture of peace programmes could have succeeded if it were just a question of the United Nations secretariat and the people in the countries concerned. However, they were defeated by the Member States in two ways. First, the rich states refused to provide funding to the 10 project profiles presented from Mozambique and all but one of the 23 project profiles presented from El Salvador, despite the fact that all of these profiles were developed jointly by the government and civil society in those countries. And second, once new governments became established in those countries, they abandoned the projects because they no longer wished to share power with the civil society.

It was through the experience of these national culture of peace programmes that I first became convinced that a culture of peace is possible. On retrospect, I now see that their partial success was due to the fact that we were working with civil society organizations in the context of failed states. As discussed below, the precedent is set for the establishment of a culture of peace when the global system of states is in failure.

We had been warned not to expect support from the powerful Member States early in our work by Alvaro de Soto. De Soto was embittered by his experience in El Salvador where he had represented the United Nations in the 1992 Chapultepec Accords that ended the civil war in that country. The US and European signatories to the treaty had promised to pay for the land reform and the judicial reform that were key points of the peace accords, but once the accords were signed, they refused to pay the money. "Why?" he asked us pointedly, "should we expect they will pay for a culture of peace?" By the way, the same thing happened to Zimbabwe after the Lancaster House Peace Accords of 1979 when the British government promised to pay for land reform as part of the agreement and later reneged on their promise.

In Mozambique, the American ambassador told me they would provide no funding for a national culture of peace programme. Instead, all aid from the United States was already earmarked so that money from the Democratic Party in the U.S. would go to the Frelimo Party in Mozambique and money from the Republican Party in the U.S. to the Renamo party in Mozambique. In effect, the

American aid was meant to corrupt the Mozambican political system in the same fashion as the U.S. political system and make it permeable to American investment.

In summary, the cause of the United Nations seems hopeless for a culture of peace as long as it is under the control of the nation-states of the world with their culture of war.

But **the culture of war is not sustainable**. This became clear when I worked during the 1970's and 1980's as a scientist in the old Soviet Union. The Soviets tried to match the West in military spending on top of an economy only half as large as the West. To do so they had to devote 80-90% of their scientists and engineers to the military, which was double the percentage in the West. Their production of useful products suffered as a result, both for the needs of their own citizens, and for their exports. Eventually, imports outstripped exports, the balance of payments became worse and worse, and finally the ruble collapsed. Meanwhile, over the years the Soviets had lost the support of their people. The same secrecy that hid the negative balance of payments was used to hide information from the public. The Russian people used to say, "You can find the news anywhere except in Izvestia and the truth anywhere except in Pravda", the government newspapers named "news" and "truth" in Russian. The combination of the disastrous war in Afghanistan and the disastrous explosion of Chernobyl destroyed what faith might otherwise have remained. Hence when the economy collapsed at the end of the 1980's, no one went to streets to save it and the military, the last resort for the culture of war, stayed in their barracks.

Now the same scenario is being played out by the American Empire. The quantity and quality of civilian goods manufactured and exported by the U.S. decreases each year as its dependence continues to rise on bases and interventions abroad and military spending at home. The U.S. has tried to hide the high proportion of military spending over the years by distributing it to separate accounts (nuclear weapons are in the Department of Energy), keeping it secret (the secret budget of the CIA) or exaggerating the size of the non-military budget (by including social security). Meanwhile, the American people have lost faith in national institutions such as the media and government. Polls in recent years have shown that confidence in government, either the Presidency, the Congress or the Supreme Court has fallen to an all-time low. The disastrous wars in Iraq and Afghanistan and the failure to protect New Orleans are destroying whatever faith might have remained. When the American economy collapses, who will go to the streets to save the government? And will the military, demoralized by Iraq and Afghanistan, leave its barracks to intervene?

History teaches us that the crises in Russia and the U.S. are not exceptions, and that state systems, being based on the culture of war, collapse from time to time. It is at the moment of such collapse that transitions become possible. For example, at the end of the two World Wars in the 20th Century, when state systems collapsed, they were replaced by revolutionary governments. Unfortunately, since these new revolutionary governments were established by movements organized according to the culture of war, the new governments were no less cultures of war than those that they replaced. Similarly, in the 1930's with the collapse of the global economy, many governments collapsed and were replaced. Unfortunately, in many cases the new states were fascist, with fascism being the extreme case of the culture of war in all respects.

Without being able to predict a precise date, we can expect within the next few decades that the American

Empire and the globalized economy associated with it will crash as did the world economy in 1929 and the Soviet economy in 1989. This time, the interdependence of states in the global economy is greater than in 1929 and we may expect massive failures of states around the world. The suffering of people will probably be greater than after 1929 because people are now much more concentrated in cities than they were a century ago. At least in the 1930's they could subsist on the family farms, but most of these farms have long since disappeared.

A global crash sets the stage for two possible political solutions which are diametrically opposite. One is a strengthening of the culture of war at the level of the state into fascism which was the predominant reaction in the 1930's. The other is the reorganization of the world's political structure to be based on cities and local governments rather than states. The latter would provide a golden opportunity for a transition to the culture of peace.

A third possibility seems unlikely according to the present analysis: the transformation of the state to a culture of peace. It is unlikely because it is not only the state that is entangled in the culture of war, but the entire structure of industry and media linked to it, the military-industrial-media complex. The roots of this structure involve far more than a simple analysis of military forces might suggest. Instead, its roots extend into the exploitative economic systems between and within nations, corruption at all levels of which the drugs for guns trade is only the most extreme, and attitudes about nationalism. Nationalist attitudes are associated with enemy images, male and racial supremacy, and the efficacy of violence and they are constantly being reinforced at all levels from the family to the media to election campaigns, to the systems of education at all levels from primary education to the universities and academic specialists. And finally, the last resort of state power is to rely on military force for the maintenance of its power. The experience of the 1930's indicates that the response to an economic crash in the absence of a viable alternative culture of peace often tends towards nationalism and the reliance on internal military force leading towards fascism.

To avoid the "fascist solution," we must continue and intensify efforts to strengthen democratic institutions and educate people to recognize the danger signs and resist the government-industrial-financial conspiracies that move a country towards authoritarian rule.

On the positive side, it is urgent to develop a global network of local governments devoted to a culture of peace so that an alternative system will be available when the state system collapses.

People ask me when the American Empire will collapse, and my response is "Much too soon, because we are not prepared for it." And I refer them to an article of Johan Galtung (2004), *On the Coming Decline and Fall of the U.S. Empire*. One takes Galtung especially seriously because in 1980 he predicted the collapse of the Soviet Empire within 10 years and he was precisely correct. In year 2000 Galtung predicted that the U.S. Empire would collapse in 2025, but in his 2004 article he says that the ill-conceived actions of President George W. Bush brings the end forward to 2020: In any case, we have little time!

My utopian novella, *I Have Seen the Promised Land* (Adams 2009), imagines a scenario of a crash of the American empire and the global economy in 2020 and a subsequent transition to a culture of peace by replacing representation of Member States on the UN Security Council by representation of local government authorities. It has been a useful exercise for me to write this scenario, and I hope that readers will find it equally useful.

Although the crash of the global economy will provide an opportunity for restructuring world government, it will also be a disaster for ordinary people. Supermarket shelves will be empty when there is no fuel for trucks to transport food and no fuel for production by agrobusiness. After the supermarket shelves are emptied (which could happen in a few days time), it will not be long before the cities are emptied of people. In the countryside, the few remaining family farms and organic cooperatives will be swamped with uninvited visitors.

Many young people have already thought about this scenario and have begun working on alternative local agriculture. These young people are a solid base on which the new culture of peace can be developed, and it is recommended that culture of peace commissions seek them out and involve them in their work.

9) WHAT WOULD A CULTURE OF PEACE BE LIKE?

The culture of peace should be understood as a process, in the original sense of the word "culture". We will not wake up one morning and find that a culture of peace has been built. My colleagues in Mozambique insisted, with good reason, on using the phrase "cultivating peace" instead of "building peace." Like agriculture, it will have its seasons of growth and harvest, and its seasons when the fields lie fallow and there seems to be no progress. And like agriculture, we must plant the seeds, help them grow by providing water and fertilizer and harvest the results in season.

With the preceding in mind, the strategy provided in this book will only provide the first steps in making possible a culture of peace. By constructing a new system of global governance that avoids state power, we will remove a great obstacle to the development of a culture of peace, but this is only a beginning.

The world will still be divided between the "haves" and the "have-nots." If anything, a global economic crash will increase this division. And ultimately a culture of peace will require economic justice, a reversal of the widening gap between rich and poor. How this will come about, we cannot yet imagine. One thing seems certain, however; it will not come about under the present system of nation-states and their culture of war.

The conclusion of the monograph that I wrote for UNESCO in 1995 called the transition to the culture of peace the most radical and far-reaching change in human history :

> "The transformation of society from a culture of war to a culture of peace is perhaps more radical and far reaching than any previous change in human history. Every aspect of social relations - having been shaped for millennia by the dominant culture of war, is open to change - from the relations among nations to those between women and men. Everyone, from the centres of power to the most remote villages, may be engaged and transformed in the process ..."

One important consequence should be a reduction of violence at the local level, including within the family. There is good scientific documentation that much of the violence at a local level is the result of the culture of war at a national or tribal level. This has been shown by both cross-national and cross-cultural anthropological studies.

The cross-national study is in the book by Dane Archer and Rosemary Gartner (1984). The authors found a strong correlation of homicide rates with warfare by the nation involved and suggested that it was caused by the state's legitimization of violence.

The cross-cultural study concerning non-state societies also showed that more war is associated with more homicide and assault. This was published by Mel and Carol Ember (1994) in the Journal of Conflict Resolution. They found significant correlation coefficients between frequency of war and individual homicide, individual assault and socially-organized homicide for non-state societies. Evidence indicates that the direction of the relationship is from war to homicide rather than the other direction. In particular, the relationship appears to be mediated by the socialization of boys for aggression in preparation for warrior roles. The researchers tested many possible explanations for high homicide and assault rates, but none were as strong as that of socialization for aggression. Further confirmation was found with the fact that if a society became pacified over time, there was a drop in the socialization for aggression, presumably because it was no longer needed to prepare for war. Looking at this process over time, it could be seen that the longer a society had been pacified, the lower its socialization for aggression, indicating that the pacification of the society was the causal factor, not vice versa.

In addition to the causal relationship of war -> socialization for aggression -> homicide and assault, the Embers also found a separate direct relationship of war -> homicide and assault. This, they suggest, may be due to the legitimization of violence by war, corresponding to the findings in the study of nation-states by Archer and Gartner quoted above. The Embers conclude that "If we want to rid the world of violence, we may first have to rid the world of war":

> "If this theory is correct, war is an important indirect cause of interpersonal violence within a society. War may also be a direct cause of more violence because war legitimizes violence. Our results imply that if we want to reduce the likelihood of interpersonal violence in our society, we may mostly need to reduce the likelihood of war, which would minimize the need to socialize for aggression and possible reduce the likelihood of all violence. War and violence appear to be causally related. If we want to rid the world of violence, we may first have to rid the world of war."

Judging from the evidence quoted above, violence at the local level may be expected to decrease under a culture of peace. This will be facilitated by a reduction in state support for the illegal trade in drugs for guns. Probably the greatest reduction in violence can be expected in the community and family once the legitimization of violence by war and by the culture of war legal system are reduced. In particular, we can expect that women and children will no longer be victims of rape and beating to the extent that they have been under the culture of war.

The reduction in violence under a culture of peace will help to reinforce culture of peace consciousness and support for local governance committed to a culture of peace. Education can be freed up from the demands of the "banking" and testing systems now in place and allowed to become "problem-solving education" in the sense of Paulo Freire. Mass media can be freed up from the present emphasis on violence and pessimism and become a vehicle for true discussion and learning. The culture of peace at the city and provincial level thus becomes a self-reinforcing process, just as at the beginning of history, the state with its culture of war became a self-reinforcing process. History itself is transformed.

The pessimism that one hears so often, that the state is necessary in order to keep in check the citizenry because human beings are naturally violent and greedy, will begin to disappear as local violence is reduced and the mass media stops exaggerating its coverage of violence. Another source of pessimism, support of the state that is based on the mistaken belief that dominance and submission is inherent in human nature will also be reduced as local governance and local economies begin to function autonomously. Leadership, in the absence of a culture of war, is not coercive. This is described in the response of the noted French anthropologist Pierre Clastres (1975) to an incredulous interviewer how the "primitive" people that he had observed in South America could exist without a state. He replied:

> "There is no coercion in primitive societies ... In our countries ... it's society that is obliged to obey the chief, while the chief has no obligations. And why doesn't the despot have any obligation? Because he has the power, naturally. That's what is meant by power in our society: 'Now the obligations are yours, not mine.' In the primitive society, it's exactly the opposite. It is only the chief who has obligations to be a good spokesman, and not only to have the talent but to prove it constantly

> by pleasing people with his discourse, by his
> obligation to be generous ..."

Clastres gives the example of a tribal leader who began to
"go crazy" and give orders for a battle that was not based on
the traditional framework of their wars, but based instead on
a personal vendetta. The tribe simply turned their back on
him and abandoned him as their leader. Losing face, the
leader committed suicide.

In fact, as Clastres stresses, it is not domination that
creates the state, but rather it is the state that creates
domination. Clastres' analysis fits very well with those of
Carneiro and others described earlier on the origins of the
state.

> "On the basis of my research and reflection
> simply in the context of primitive society, it
> seems to me that the state does not develop after
> the division of society into opposing social
> groups or classes or after the division of rich and
> poor, exploiters and exploited. Instead, the
> primary division and that from which all the
> others follow, is the division between those who
> command and those who obey, in others words,
> the state. Fundamentally, that is where it comes
> from, the division of society between those who
> have power and those who submit to power."

As the culture of peace gets established, we may
expect a great release of human creativity and problem-
solving, supported by a renewed educational system and
mass media. Freed from the constraints of a culture of war,
problems that seem unsolvable today become more
amenable to solution. With the removal of the obstacles that
came from the culture of war, the various social movements

should make great progress toward disarmament, universal human rights, democratic participation, equality of women, sustainable development, etc. Take, for example, the two risks that seem at the present time to endanger all life on the planet: the risk of nuclear war; and the process of global warming as a result of burning fossil fuels.

The risk of nuclear war has been maintained by the insistence of powerful nation-states to produce weapons-grade uranium and make and stockpile nuclear weapons, but this, too, can be overcome. Once power passes from the state to local authorities, there will be no further reason to make or keep nuclear weapons, and the disarmament procedures already tried and tested at the end of the Cold War can be used to rid the world once and for all of this terrible threat. The International Atomic Energy Agency, whose hands have been tied by political pressures throughout its history, would finally be able to manage and verify its fundamental task of nuclear disarmament.

Overcoming global warming is a complex task, but will become simpler as soon as decision-making powers devolve to local authorities. As we have seen the leadership for conversion to renewable energy comes from local authorities and local initiatives, and this can be expected to intensify after the transition to a culture of peace, especially if local economies have been developed that do not exploit fossil fuels and destroy other environmental resources such as forests. Local authorities are in the best position to accomplish the energy conservation, renewable energy sources, reforestation and other such measures that can reverse the increasing atmospheric concentration of carbon dioxide. With the development of a culture of peace, it will finally be possible to establish an international coordinating mechanism for sustainable development, something that has been blocked in the past by the Member States of the United Nations.

The transition to a culture of peace can finally begin to reverse the constantly increasing gap between rich and poor, that has grown to such destructive proportions, both between rich and poor countries and between rich and poor within each country.   Here, too, much depends on the progress made in local economies that are not exploitative, neither of the environment nor of agricultural and industrial workers.

Once the gap between rich regions and poor regions of the world begins to shrink, the solution will be found to the "brain drain" which presently contributes to that gap. The brightest young students from poor regions of the world may still go to the rich regions for their education, but will now be more likely to return to the regions of their birth, bringing with them scientific methods and global communication links that can enrich their home communities. This will finally present the solution to the present mass migrations of people from the poverty-stricken South to the historically rich North that has provoked xenophobic and demagogic political movements in the Northern countries. Such a vision was provided in a speech to UNESCO by a former African President:

> He looked forward to a new era in which the young men and women from the villages in his region of Africa would go away to school and university in the North, would learn the world's accumulated wisdom and make friends of other youth from around the world. Then they would return to live in their native villages, bringing a computer with which they could stay in touch with their friends and with the world's

knowledge. They would help apply this knowledge to the practices of the village, for example in medical and farming techniques, and this would all take place within the traditional social and economic framework of the village.

The emphasis on local economies could redress the historical gap between rural and urban life. It could reinvigorate family and village farming, bringing people back to rural life without losing the communication and transportation amenities now available only to urban dwellers. Family and village-based farming encourages reconstitution of the extended family which has been devastated in recent decades, which provides a milieu in which the elderly, the handicapped and children have a place of honor, respect and love. It also provides an answer to the growing health hazards of obesity due to lack of any meaningful physical labor for urban dwellers. There is a joy in farming that is hard to describe unless you have experienced it. From my own boyhood days working on farms in the Ozarks and in California I remember with pleasure the hard physical work of splitting rails, going after the cows on horseback, planting, irrigating, cultivating, harvesting, bucking bales, slaughtering (with a prayer of thanks), milking cows, and, yes, even shoveling fresh manure. The relation with the land, with the animals and with the growing plants had a quality that was truly sacred. It is a joy that is shared between generations as the young learn from the old. As described in the African vision cited above, it should be possible to share in this process without losing touch with rest of the world through the use of modern technology.

The global perspective, so essential to the overcoming of enemy images, can be expanded by culture of peace tourism and educational exchange programs, to the extent that these may become the most important investment that people make with surplus from their labor. Here, too, the culture of peace becomes a self-reinforcing process.

In summary, the dawning of a culture of peace can bring a new stage of human history, in which historical process is in the hands of the people. This vision is described in the conclusion of my 1995 UNESCO monograph:

> "In the vision of a culture of peace, the very process of history itself is transformed. Freed from the culture of war, where history has unfolded on the basis of violent change in a cycle of suppression and explosion, it can move forward without violence. Instead of being determined by the few, the course of history can be determined by the participation of the many. Instead of being determined from the top down, it can be determined by changes and methods which come from the bottom up, beginning at a local level which is tied to a global consciousness. Under these conditions, the determining factor in history can become the social consciousness of the people themselves."

REFERENCES

Adams, D. (1979) Brain Mechanisms for Offense, Defense and Submission, *Behavioral and Brain Sciences*, 2: 201-241. Available on the Internet at http://www.culture-of-peace.info/bbs/title-page.html

Adams, D. (1983). Why There Are So Few Women Warriors. *Behavior Science Research.* 18 (3): 196-212. Available on the Internet at http://www.culture-of-peace.info/women/title-page.html

Adams, D. (1984). There is no instinct for war. *Psychological Journal (Moscow):* 5: 140-144 (translated from Russian and available on the Internet at http://www.culture-of-peace.info/instinct/title-page.html

Adams, D. (1985). *The American Peace Movements.* Available only on the Internet at http://www.culture-of-peace.info/apm/title-page.html

Adams, D. (1987). *Psychology for Peace Activists.* Available only on the Internet at http://www.culture-of-peace.info/ppa/title-page.html

Adams, D. and S. Bosch (1987). The myth that war is intrinsic to human nature discourages action for peace by young people. In: *Essays in Violence*, edited by J. Martin Ramirez, Robert A. Hinde and Jo Groebel, Universidad de Sevilla, Spain. Available on the Internet at http://www.culture-of-peace.info/myth/title-page.html

Adams, D. (1989). The Seville Statement on Violence: A Progress Report. *Journal of Peace Research* 26 (2): 113-121. Available on the Internet at http://www.culture-of-peace.info/ssov/title-page.html

132

Adams, D. (1990) Planning for Peace in New Haven. *Bulletin of Municipal Foreign Policy*: Summer 1990, p. 32.

Adams, D. (1991). *The Seville Statement on Violence: Preparing the Ground for the Constructing of Peace.* UNESCO. Available on Internet at http://www.culture-of-peace.info/brochure/titlepage.html

Adams, D. (1992). Biology does not make men more aggressive than women. In *Of Mice and Women: Aspects of Female Aggression*, edited by K. Bjorkvist and P. Niemela, Academic Press, Inc., Pages 17-25. Available on the Internet at http://www.culture-of-peace.info/biology/title-page.html

Adams, D. (1995). Internal Military Interventions in the United States. *Journal of Peace Research*, 32 (2): 197-211. Available on the Internet at http://www.culture-of-peace.info/intervention/title-page.html

Adams, D. (1995). *UNESCO and a Culture of Peace: Promoting a Global Movement*, original edition out of print. Available only on the Internet at http://www.culture-of-peace.info/monograph/page1.html

Adams, D. (2003). *Early History of the Culture of Peace: A Personal Memoire.* Available only on Internet at http://www.culture-of-peace.info/history/introduction.html

Adams, D. (2003). *The Aggression Systems.* Available only on Internet at http://www.culture-of-peace.info/aggression-intro.html

Adams, D. (2008) *The History of the Culture of War.* Available for reading on-line or mail-order at http://culture-of-peace.info/books/history.html

Adams, D (2009) *I Have Seen the Promised Land: A Utopian Novella.* Available for reading on-line or mail-order at http://culture-of-peace.info/books/promisedland.html

Aptheker, H. (1943). *American Negro Slave Revolts*, International Publishers, New York.

Archer, D. and R. Gartner. (1984). *Violence and Crime in Cross-National Perspective,* Yale University Press.

Boston Indicators Project (2008). *Public Safety.* Available on the Internet at http://www.bostonindicators.org/indicatorsproject/publicsafety/default.aspx

Brownmiller, S. (1975). *Against Our Will.* Simon and Schuster.

Cabezudo, A. (2007). De la ciudad educativa a la ciudad educadora, *Revista Novamerica*, No. 114, available at http://www.novamerica.org.br/Revista_digital/L0114/rev_construindo02.asp

Cabezudo, A. (2008). Argumentos y estrategias para la construcción de la ciudad educador. In: *Educando para la Paz en y desde la Universidad: Antología Conmemorativa de una Década*, Universidad de Puerto Rico, Facultad de Educación. available on the Internet at http://unescopaz.uprrp.edu/antologia.pdf

Carneiro, R. L. (1970). A Theory of the Origin of the State. *Science*, New Series, 169 (3947): 733-738.

City of São Paulo (2008). *Interurban System for Monitoring Human Rights.* Available on the Internet at http://www9.prefeitura.sp.gov.br/simdh

134

Clastres, P. (1975). Entretien avec Pierre Clastres. N°9 de la revue *L'Anti-Mythes*. Available on the Internet at http://www.plusloin.org/textes/clastres.pdf . Excerpts translated here by David Adams.

Comitê Paulista para a Década da Cultura de Paz (2001-2010). *Histórico.* Available on the Internet at http://www.comitepaz.org.br/hist%C3%B3rico.htm

Cooper, J. M. (1980). *The Army and Civil Disorder.* Westport, CT: Greenwood.

Council of Europe (2005). *Concerted Development of Social Cohesion Indicators.* Available on the Internet at http://www.coe.int/t/dg3/socialpolicies/socialcohesiondev/source/GUIDE_en.pdf

Culture of Peace News Network. Website on the Internet at http://www.cpnn-world.org

DeRivera, J.H. (2004) Assessing the basis for a culture of peace in contemporary societies. *Journal of Peace Research* 41,531-548.

Derthick, M. (1965). *The National Guard in Politics.* Cambridge, MA: Harvard University Press.

Earth Charter in Action. Website on the Internet at http://www.earthcharterinaction.org/about_charter.shtml

Ember, C. R. and M. Ember (2007). War and the Socialization of Children: Comparing Two Evolutionary Models. *Cross-Cultural Research* 41: 96-122.

Ember, M. and C. R. Ember (1994). War, Socialization, and Interpersonal Violence: A Cross-Cultural Study. *Journal of Conflict Resolution.* 38: 620-646.

Ember, M. and C. R. Ember (2001). Making the World More Peaceful: Policy Implications of Cross-Cultural Research. In *Prevention and control of aggression and the impact on its victims,* Manuela Martinez, ed. New York: Kluwer/Plenum, 331-338.

Federation of Canadian Municipalities (2004) *A City Tailored to Women: The Role of Municipal Governments in Achieving Gender Equality.* Available on the Internet at http://www.euroafricanpartnership.org/contributi/a_city_tail ored.pdf

Freire, P. (1968). *Pedagogy of the Oppressed.* Continuum International Publishing Group. Excerpts available on the Internet at http://www.zonalatina.com/Zldata288.htm

Friends Committee on National Legislation (2008). Where do our income tax dollars go? Available on Internet at http://www.fcnl.org/pdfs/taxDay08.pdf

Galtung, J. (1996). *Peace by Peaceful Means.* Sage Publications, Inc.

Galtung, J. (2004). *On the Coming Decline and Fall of the US Empire.* Available on the Internet at http://www.transnational.org/SAJT/forum/meet/2004/Galtun g_USempireFall.html

Gandhi, M. (1929). *The Story of My Experiments with Truth: Gandhi's Life in His Own Words.* Excerpts available on the Internet at http://www.navajivantrust.org/gandhilife.htm

136

Georgetown University Political Database of the Americas (2007). Proyecto Democracia y Seguridad Ciudadana. Available on the Internet at: http://pdba.georgetown.edu/Security/citizensecurity/Brazil/documents/Indicadores_Brazil.pdf

Global Peace Index (2007). Available on the Internet at http://visionofhumanity.com

Grossman, D. (1995). *On Killing: The Psychological Cost of Learning to Kill in War and Society*, Little Brown and Co. Boston.

Heider, K. G. (1979). *Grand Valley Dani: Peaceful Warriors*. Holt, Rinehart and Winston, Inc.

Human Security Policy Division at Foreign Affairs and International Trade Canada (2007). *Human Security for an Urban Century: Local Challenges, Global Perspectives.* Available on the Internet at http://humansecurity-cities.org/sites/hscities/files/Human_Security_for_an_Urban_Century.pdf

International Council for Local Environmental Initiatives. Website on the Internet at http://www.iclei.org . Including article entitled *Orienting Urban Planning to Sustainability in Curitiba, Brazil* at http://www3.iclei.org/localstrategies/summary/curitiba2.html

International Observatory on Participatory Democracy (2006). *Practical Guide For Evaluating Participatory Processes.* Available on the Internet at http://www.oidp.net/pdf/GuiaPracticaEvaluacion_en.pdf

International Peace Bureau,. Website on the Internet at http://www.ipb.org

Jaspers, K. (1953). *The Origin and Goal of History*, translated by Michael Bullock, New Haven, CT: Yale University Press.

King, M. L. (1968). Honoring Dr. Du Bois. *Freedomways,* Second Quarter 1968, 104-111.

Lacayo Parajon, F., M. Lourenço and D. Adams. (1996). The Unesco Culture Of Peace Programme in El Salvador: An Initial Report. *The International Journal of Peace Studies.* 1 (2): 1-20. Available on the Internet at http://www.gmu.edu/academic/ijps/vol1_2/UNESCO.htm

Lerner, J. and Schugurensky, D. (2005). Learning Citizenship and Democracy through Participatory Budgeting: The Case of Rosario, Argentina. Available at: http://www.linesofflight.net/work/rosario_pb_columbia.pdf

Mahon, J. K. (1983). *History of the Militia and the National Guard*. Macmillan, New York.

Mandela, N. (1994). *Long Walk to Freedom*. Little, Brown and Company.

Manifesto 2000. Available only on Internet at http://www3.unesco.org/iycp/uk/uk_sum_manifesto2000.htm

Mozambique (1994). Draft Culture of Peace Programme. Available on the Internet at http://www.culture-of-peace.info/annexes/mozambique/cover.html

138

Nkrumah, K. (1965). *Neo-Colonialism, the Last Stage of Imperialism.* Available on the Internet at http://www.marxists.org/subject/africa/nkrumah/neo-colonialism/ch01.htm

Nobel Peace Prize (1977). Presentation Speech to the Amnesty International. Available on the Internet at http://nobelprize.org/nobel_prizes/peace/laureates/1977/press.html

Nobel Peace Prize (1997). Presentation Speech to the International Campaign to Ban Landmines. Available at: http://nobelprize.org/nobel_prizes/peace/laureates/1997/presentation-speech.html

Oxfam America (2001). *Cuba: Going Against the Grain,* Available on the Internet at http://www.oxfamamerica.org/newsandpublications/publications/research_reports/art1164.html

Participatory Budgeting. Website on the Internet at http://www.participatorybudgeting.org/Whatis.htm

Reardon, B. A. (1985). *Sexism and the War System.* Columbia University Press, New York.

Reporters Without Frontiers. (2007). *Annual Press Freedom Survey.* Summary available on the Internet at http://www.rsf.org/rubrique.php3?id_rubrique=659

Riker, W. H. (1957). *The Role of the National Guard in American Democracy.* Washington, DC: Public Affairs Press.

Roche, D. (2003). *The Human Right to Peace.* Ottawa: Novalis.

Seville Statement on Violence (1986). Available at http://portal.unesco.org/education/en/ev.php-URL_ID=3247&URL_DO=DO_TOPIC&URL_SECTION=201.html

Seville Statement on Violence Newsletter. (March 2003) available only on Internet at http://www.culture-of-peace.info/SSOVnews303/page2.html

Sipes, R. G. (1973). War, sports, and aggression: An empirical test of two rival theories. *American Anthropologist* 75: 64-86.

Stearns, C. and Stearns, P. (1989) *Anger: The Struggle for Emotional Control in America's History.* University of Chicago Press.

Transparency International España (2008) Indice de Transparencia de los Ayuntamientos 2008. Available on the Internet at http://www.transparencia.org.es/

UNESCO (1945). *Constitution.* Available on the Internet at http://unesdoc.unesco.org/images/0012/001255/125590e.pdf #page=7

UNESCO (1960). *All Men Are Brothers: Quotations from Gandhi.*

UNESCO (1992). *Co-operation to promote a culture of peace.* Executive Board Document 140 EX/28. Available on the Internet at http://www.culture-of-peace.info/annexes/140ex28/coverpage.html

UNESCO (1994). *History of Humanity. Volumes I-VII.* Routledge Publishing.

140

UNESCO (1996) Sintra Plan of Action. Available on the Internet at http://portal.unesco.org/education/en/ev.php-URL_ID=3216&URL_DO=DO_TOPIC&URL_SECTION=201.html

UNESCO (1999). Fifth Commission of the UNESCO General Conference of 1999, unofficial record available on the Internet at http://www.culture-of-peace.info/annexes/commissionV/summary.html

United for Peace and Justice. Website on the Internet at http://www.unitedforpeace.org/

United Cities and Local Governments. Website on the Internet at http://www.cities-localgovernments.org

United Nations (1946). *Charter of the United Nations.* Available on the Internet at http://www.un.org/aboutun/charter/index.html

United Nations (1948). *The Universal Declaration of Human Rights.* Available on the Internet at http://www.un.org/Overview/rights.html

United Nations (1992). *An Agenda for Peace: Preventive diplomacy, peacemaking and peace-keeping.* Document A/47/277. Available on the Internet at: http://www.un.org/Docs/SG/agpeace.html

United Nations (1998). *Consolidated report containing a draft declaration and programme of action on a culture of peace.* Document A/53/370. Available on Internet at http://www.culture-of-peace.info/annexes/resA-53-370/coverpage.html

United Nations (1999). *Declaration and Programme of Action on a Culture of Peace. Document A/53/243.* Available on Internet at : http://www3.unesco.org/iycp/uk/uk_sum_refdoc.htm

United Nations (2000). *Report of the Secretary-General: International Decade for a Culture of Peace and Non-Violence for the Children of the World.* A/55/377. Available on the Internet at http://www3.unesco.org/iycp/uk/uk_sum_refdoc.htm

United States Department of State (2001). *World Military Expenditures and Arms Transfers 1999-2000.* Available at: http://www.fas.org/man/docs/wmeat9900/table1.pdf

Weber, M. (1921). Politics as a Vocation. In *From Max Weber: Essays in Sociology,* edited by H. H. Gerth and C. Wright Mills, 77-128. New York: Oxford University Press.

White, L. A. (1959). *The Evolution of Culture.* New York: McGraw-Hill.

Wikipedia Free Encyclopedia. Available on Internet at http://en.wikipedia.org/wiki/Main_Page

World Civil Society Report on the Culture of Peace (2005). Available on the Internet at http://decade-culture-of-peace.org

World Culture of Peace Index (2000). Available at: http://www.dhseol.org/publish/archive/wcpi_2000.pdf

Youth for Culture of Peace. (2006). Available at: http://decade-culture-of-peace.org/report/YouthReport.pdf

INDEX

144

146

2903012

Made in the USA